YORK NOTES

Beloved

Toni Morrison

Notes by Laura Gray

Longman   York Press

YORK PRESS
322 Old Brompton Road, London SW5 9JH

PEARSON EDUCATION LIMITED
Edinburgh Gate, Harlow,
Essex CM20 2JE, United Kingdom
Associated companies, branches and representatives throughout the world

© Librairie du Liban *Publishers* 1999

First published 1999
Sixth impression 2003

ISBN 0–582–41460–1

Designed by Vicki Pacey, Trojan Horse, London
Phototypeset by Gem Graphics, Trenance, Mawgan Porth, Cornwall
Colour reproduction and film output by Spectrum Colour
Produced by Pearson Education Asia Limited, Hong Kong

ONTENTS

PART FOUR

TEXTUAL ANALYSIS

PART FIVE

BACKGROUND

PART SIX

CRITICAL HISTORY AND BROADER PERSPECTIVES

PART ONE

INTRODUCTION

HOW TO STUDY A NOVEL

Studying a novel on your own requires self-discipline and a carefully thought-out work plan in order to be effective.

- You will need to read the novel more than once. Start reading it quickly for pleasure, then read it slowly and thoroughly.
- On your second reading make detailed notes on the plot, characters and themes of the novel. Further readings will generate new ideas and help you to memorise the details of the story
- Some of the characters will develop as the plot unfolds. How do your responses towards them change during the course of the novel?
- Think about how the novel is narrated. From whose point of view are events described?
- A novel may or may not present events chronologically: the time scheme may be a key to its structure and organisation.
- What part do the settings play in the novel?
- Are words, images or incidents repeated so as to give the work a pattern? Do such patterns help you to understand the novel's themes?
- Identify what styles of language are used in the novel.
- What is the effect of the novel's ending? Is the action completed and closed, or left incomplete and open?
- Does the novel present a moral and just world?
- Cite exact sources for all quotations, whether from the text itself or from critical commentaries. Wherever possible find your own examples from the novel to back up your opinions.
- Always express your ideas in your own words.

This York Note offers an introduction to *Beloved* and cannot substitute for close reading of the text and the study of secondary sources.

Beloved examines America's past of slavery and is dedicated to the 'Sixty Million and More' Africans who died in the Middle Passage on the slave ships to America. In an interview in *Race Today Review*, 1985, Toni Morrison tells us her main aim in writing this novel was to 'bear witness to a history that is unrecorded, untaught in mainstream education'.

She has to a great extent relied on oral history, and attempted to replicate the black female slave's voice, her 'unspeakable thoughts, unspoken' (p. 199). The result is a new kind of history, melding and interlocking different accounts and versions of events, to create an emotional, fictional response to slavery. *Beloved* is a ghost story, a love story, an examination of what it means to 'be-loved', a political novel, an African-American novel and a novel for feminism and for humanity. It has a rich, many-layered structure which generates as many interpretations and readings as its **eponymous** character. It is universal in its appeal: the mysterious style and lyrical beauty combine with messages and images that maul the reader's sensibility and conscience, making it a complex novel that is at times difficult and painful to read, but always rewarding.

The plot of *Beloved* is not easy to summarise. Toni Morrison's technique is to thread various narratives together, using the present tense to convey the vividness of the memories of her characters. *Beloved* is the story of a visitation from the past and the consequent upheaval in the emotional lives of its characters. It is set during an appalling period in America's history: the years of the Civil War and of slavery. After the Civil War ended, in the latter half of the nineteenth century, life was still dreadful for black people, whether slaves or freed. The novel examines the impact of slavery on a group of black people.

Beloved is a source of comment for all kinds of readers: black and white, those who read for pleasure, and those who study the text for academic ends. It is interesting to feminists, due to its focus on women and motherhood, and to students of African-American studies, both for its subject matter and its portrayal of the development and the value of community to black society. The issue of mother love and the implicit questioning of a mother's right to kill her child is itself topical in a moment in which many countries are torn by their reactions to abortion.

Toni Morrison is a writer conscious of her intent and its effect. In her sure hands, the reader of *Beloved* enjoys her terrible story.

PART TWO

SUMMARIES & COMMENTARIES

Beloved *was first published in 1987 by Knopf, New York. The edition used in preparing this guide, and to which the page references refer, is the UK Vintage paperback edition published in 1997 by Random House, UK Ltd.*

SYNOPSIS

Sethe, the **protagonist** of the novel, is a slave on a farm in Kentucky called Sweet Home. The other slaves who belong to the farm are three half-brothers – Paul A, Paul D and Paul F – and two other men, Sixo and Halle. The latter becomes Sethe's husband. While their owner Mr Garner is alive, the slaves enjoy a relatively stable way of life. Garner prides himself on treating his slaves as men. He allows them to use guns and to hunt to supplement their rations and he lets them choose their own partners, rather than breeding from them for offspring. Unfortunately, he dies unexpectedly and Sweet Home is taken over by his brother-in-law, schoolteacher. Schoolteacher regards slaves as animals and, aided by his nephews, submits them to various investigations and experiments. He will not allow them to use guns and ties up Sixo for having killed a young pig.

As the quality of their lives deteriorates, the slaves decide to escape. Paul D and Sethe are the only two who succeed. The other Pauls are killed, and Sixo is shot when the white men are unable to burn him alive. Halle witnesses Sethe's rape and beating by schoolteacher's nephews, and is reduced to a wreck. We assume that he also dies. Paul D is sold and spends several months in a prison camp in Georgia because he attempted to kill his new master. He manages to escape with the other members of the chain gang.

Sethe, heavily pregnant with her fourth child, sends her other three children ahead to her mother-in-law's house and runs away. She survives the journey and is helped by a white girl. She gives birth to her second daughter, Denver, on the banks of the Ohio. Helped by Ella and Stamp Paid, two black people who assist runaways, she arrives at Halle's mother's house in Cincinnati and is reunited with her other children. Halle's mother is known as Baby Suggs: she used to live at Sweet Home until Halle bought her freedom. In Cincinnati she has become an unofficial preacher and a significant figure in the local black community.

After only twenty-eight days of stolen liberty, schoolteacher comes to retrieve Sethe. Rather than allow her four children to submit to the sexual abuse, exploitation and indignity that she has had to suffer, she takes them to the woodshed and tries to kill them. She intends to commit suicide herself. She is successful in despatching only one of her children to 'safety' – her eldest girl, whose throat she cuts. The two boys, Howard and Buglar, survive, run away. Sethe is prevented from smashing Denver's head against the wall. She goes to prison with Denver and is saved from being hanged by the exertions of the Bodwins and various societies in favour of the abolition of slavery. These facts only appear as the narrative unfolds.

Beloved begins almost twenty years after these events are supposed to have happened. Sethe is still living in the house on 124 Bluestone Road with Denver. The two women are ostracised by the black community. Baby Suggs has died. The house is rocked by the spite of the murdered baby girl's ghost, who engages in poltergeist activities; it is saturated with an atmosphere of misery, manifested in pools of red light. In the first section Sethe wishes that her daughter would come back and allow her to explain her dramatic action. The novel charts this very event. A girl arrives whom Sethe and Denver gradually come to accept as the ghost made flesh. She calls herself Beloved – the name engraved on the toddler's gravestone. The other inhabitant of 124 Bluestone Road is Paul D, who arrives to visit Sethe. He and Sethe have a relationship and he is as antagonistic towards the living Beloved, as he was to the ghost, whom he banished from the house on the day of his arrival. Denver, who has been lonely for many years, is dependent on Beloved, and resentful of Paul D.

Stamp Paid decides to tell Paul D of Sethe's crime and the period that she spent in prison. Paul D is awed and repelled by Sethe's reaction to the realities of black existence, and leaves the house.

After his departure, Sethe is positive that Beloved is her daughter and slowly relinquishes everyday life. She loses her job in a restaurant and spends each day trying to compensate and justify herself to Beloved. The three women lock themselves into the house in a deadlock of love, blame and guilt. Beloved grows fatter and fatter while Sethe shrinks away to nothing. Denver realises that she must do something, and braves the outside world to look for a job. She is waiting to be collected by her new employer, when the women of the area come to Sethe's rescue. They have heard of the presence of the ghost and are determined to rid the house of Beloved. As they are gathered outside, Mr Bodwin appears. He is a white man who has helped three consecutive generations of Baby Suggs's family, and arrives to pick up Denver. Sethe lunges at him with an ice-pick, convinced that he is another danger to her children, but is struck by one of the other women. Beloved disappears.

Later Paul D comes to visit Sethe and finds her lying in Baby Suggs's bed. He washes her and tells her that their shared past must be overcome. She must stop grieving for the death of her child and begin to value herself. The novel ends with the possibility of a future life for Sethe, Denver and Paul D. There is an epilogue which commemorates the way in which the novel's **protagonists** forget their supernatural visitation.

DETAILED SUMMARIES & COMMENTARIES

PRELIMINARY PAGES

These pages contain quotations which have great bearing on the text.

Sixty Million and more those slaves who died on the long voyage from Africa to America. Morrison dedicates her novel to the dead

I will call them ... this passage (from Romans 9:25) draws out the **irony** of the name of one of the protagonists. Beloved is called into being by her mother, Sethe, and the novel is named after her. The issue of calling and identity is central. By citing a New Testament passage which repeats with little difference an Old Testament one, Morrison creates uncertainty about the relationship between past and present

ONE

SECTION 1 PAGES 3–9

> **Paul D appears at 124 Bluestone Road. Denver feels
> threatened. Paul D and Sethe begin to piece together
> details of the failed escape from Sweet Home. The
> poltergeist protests and Paul D reacts by beating it out of
> the house. Sethe and Paul D retire upstairs**

The year is 1873, and the place 124 Bluestone Road, in Ohio. The
house is inhabited by Sethe and her two daughters: one is the eighteen-
year-old Denver, the other the spirit of a toddler known as Beloved.
Sethe wishes that Beloved could appear, so that she would have the
opportunity to explain everything to her. Previously Sethe's mother-in-
law, Baby Suggs, also lived there. Her death and a few fragments of her
life are recounted. She had had eight children: 'four taken, four
chased'. Sethe tells us that Baby Suggs took to her bed and to 'pondering
color', some nine years ago. Sethe and her 'girl Denver', aged ten,
try to summon up the baby ghost shortly after Baby Suggs has died.
Sethe's two sons, Howard and Buglar, also lived in 124, but ran away
before they were thirteen because of the spite of the ghost. The house is
avoided; neighbours gallop past and there are very few visitors and
even fewer friends. We hear about the pink-flecked stone of Beloved's
grave and learn that her throat was cut. Sethe pays for the wording
on the headstone by having sex with the stone-mason.

Sethe arrives home to find Paul D who has not seen her for
nineteen years. They used to work as slaves on an estate called Sweet
Home. As Sethe makes bread she explains that she has a 'tree' on her
back, composed of scars from a brutal beating. She escaped from Sweet
Home while she was pregnant with Denver. She was 'nursed' by two
white boys who stole the milk from her swollen breasts. Her other three
children, Beloved, Howard and Buglar, were already on their way to stay
with Baby Suggs in 124. A 'whitegirl' helped her. Her husband and the
father of her children – Halle –and Paul D were two of five men who
'belonged' to Sweet Home and its proprietors, the Garners. As black
people they were possessions: Sethe herself was a 'timely present' compensating for the loss of Baby Suggs, whom Halle bought out of slavery.

As Paul D walks into the house he is conscious of 'evil', and feels the sadness that possesses the house. Denver is excluded from the shared memories of her mother and Paul D. She feels as lonely and rebuked as she claims the ghost is, denied the company of her brothers and of other children. She tells Sethe that she cannot live in the house any more. She cries, and later so does her mother. Paul D holds Sethe and kisses her scarred back. As a consequence, the house is rocked by the ghost. Paul D reacts to its presence and throws the furniture about, shouting at the spirit. Denver is half-exalted by the emanation, but is left eating burnt bread and jam from a broken jar as her mother and the stranger go upstairs to make love.

This opening section presents many of the events which are later unravelled in the novel. The time-scale is elastic. References are elliptic: coherence is denied and details are given that will only be contextualised during the course of the novel. The unfolding and disintegration of Sweet Home, Sethe's escape, Denver's birth and Sethe's act of infanticide are 'stories', remembered narratives, that start here and are developed throughout the course of the novel.

The reader has to accept the supernatural presence in 124 from the very first page. Despite the pointed clues in the narrative we cannot be sure about the exact identity of Beloved, we do not know the baby girl's real name: Beloved is only the name on the gravestone, based on the minister's address at the funeral service – 'Dearly Beloved'.

The **multi-accentuality** of language, the fact that words, according to context and speaker can have different meanings, is exemplified. Paul D feels 'bad' (p. 7), Sweet Home was neither sweet nor home (p. 13) and the tree on Sethe's back is a network of scars. The loving description of Sethe's baking (pp. 16–17) while she tells Paul D about the atrocities she has had to withstand, is a terrible **juxtaposition**. The imagery of milk is one that is present throughout the novel (see Recurring Themes and Imagery).

Morrison builds up Sethe and Paul D, with metal imagery. Sethe has 'iron eyes and backbone to match' (p. 9) and her back is described as the handiwork of an ironsmith. In later sections, Paul

D is characterised by the **symbolic** tin box that has replaced his heart. This is coupled with an undercurrent of references to economic exchange and debt. As Sethe exclaims: 'I paid for the ticket ... it cost too much!' (p. 15). Sethe pays for the headstone with sex and later describes the act in these terms (p. 184). Stamp Paid, his name testifying to his 'debtlessness' (p. 185), the story of Denver's birth that makes her feel as if she has a 'bill ... owing' (p. 77), or Paul D, referring to the price of having 'bought' time by asking Sethe to get pregnant (p. 129). These two sets of images have links to the novel's historical context of slavery. The metal **metaphorically** implies the physical and spiritual bondage that Sethe and Paul D have endured, and that they carry with them in terms of physical and psychological scars. The sense of debt and price is linked with having been perceived as a human commodity, subject to valuation and sale.

124 the number of the house in the street

as soon as merely ... in the cake these are unfriendly manifestations made by the spirit that possesses the house

pondering color it will become clear later that Baby Suggs is now noticing the colour of things for the first time in her life

Ohio a north central state of America

the outrageous behavior of that place the behaviour of the unfriendly spirit

slop jars containers for dirty water etc. – the house would not have had an indoor drain

rutting mating

abolitionist an advocate for the abolition of slavery

palsied convulsed, shaking. Palsy is a human sickness – the house has taken on human qualities

chamomile a wild aromatic herb

washboard a corrugated wooden board for rubbing washing against

Boys hanging ... sycamores reference to lynchings

soughing swaying and murmuring in the wind

Can't baby feet can't pamper feet

looking for velvet obscure here but explained in Section 3 where the white girl Amy who rescues Sethe is on her way to Boston to buy velvet

Negroes in the nineteenth century a polite word for black (now derogatory)

had sold his brother sold him as a slave

bedding dress bridal attire for the wedding night

stroppin strapping

niggers (derogatory) blacks

Halle bought ... years of Sundays Halle worked on Sundays for years to buy his mother's, Baby Suggs's, freedom

speaker kind of lay preacher

hazelnut man man with light brown skin

Rebuked an obsolete meaning of rebuked is repressed. The ghost can be read as a repressed memory which Sethe has to confront and exorcise

kindlin kindling wood for lighting a fire

a look of snow an icy look

haint a spirit, a spook

the keeping room parlour or sitting room

smoking papers cigarette papers

chokecheiiy tree a sour cherry tree native to America

They used cowhide on you they used a cowhide whip

jelly (American) jam

die-witch! stories children's stories and incantations to banish evil spirits

SECTION 2 PAGES 20-7

Paul D and Sethe have sex. They lie next to each other in bed and remember Sweet Home

Sethe and Paul D have sex, hardly having time to take their clothes off, and lie next to each other, embarrassed and shy at their abandonment. Paul D is repelled by the flabby breasts which he had supported so reverently before, and disgusted by the scars on Sethe's back. Paul D remembers one of the other Sweet Home men, Sixo, who used to walk thirty miles to meet his 'woman', often leaving him with only an hour with her before he had to set off home again. Later in this same section we hear of another of Sixo's encounters with 'Patsy the Thirty-Mile Woman'.

Sethe thinks about the significance of her house, which Paul D had suggested she leave. She too remembers Sweet Home and the way in which she used to personalise the kitchen of her owner, Mrs Garner, with sprigs of flowers and herbs. We learn more about Baby Suggs's eight children, the nature of their six fathers, and the way in which the dual systems of slavery and racism affected the lives of black people. The one child she was allowed to keep was Halle, who worked on Sundays in order to pay for her freedom. Baby Suggs regards Sethe's attempts to make a home of Sweet Home with cynicism: 'A bigger fool never lived' (p. 24). Paul D gazes at Sethe, who, with her eyes shut, seems more manageable. He remembers how much he and the other Sweet Home men, with the exception of Sixo, had wanted to be with her. Sethe, conscious of his glance, remembers that she only used to see her husband in daylight on Sunday mornings. She recalls her desire for a ceremony when she first decided to marry him. Aged fourteen, she made a dress secretly, after asking Mrs Garner's permission to get married.

This section closes with the memory of Sethe's first 'coupling' with Halle, in a cornfield, as a gesture of consideration to the other men but, for all their thoughtfulness, the moving corn on a windless day made what they were doing obvious. The men feasted on the broken corn cobs that evening.

An example of Morrison's narrative technique and use of time and memory is that in the midst of Sethe's ruminations she makes a reference to Sixo's last laugh (p. 23). This fact actually belongs to Paul D's memories, and the reader only understands this reference later (p. 226), although it is referred to many times before then. This anticipation of future memories and the idea of shared consciousness: 'Her story was bearable because it was his as well – to tell, refine, to tell again' (p. 99), is a significant element of Morrison's style.

When Sethe recollects her first sexual encounter with Halle, here, her memories are joined by Paul D's thoughts as he lies beside her in bed. No speech is reported, yet their thoughts coincide and overlap, and, emphasised by the choral repetitions of a key-phrase – 'How loose the silk (p. 27), attain an eerie significance. The corn cob is also a sexual image. The phrase: 'jailed down … jailed up', describing the way in which the juice streamed down, and the way in which the same free-flowing juice has been imprisoned, with contrasting connotations of enclosure and freedom, draws attention to a larger scheme of repetition in the passage. We are once again in Paul D's consciousness, signified by 'he'. The next paragraph recounts the reflections of a female character, who, we assume, is Sethe, convinced that the preparation of corn is painful. The passage closes with a reference to 'you'. The reader is aware that they are still sharing the thoughts of a character, but it is impossible to be sure to whom these thoughts belong, or to whom they are addressed. The psychic union between Paul D and Sethe follows their sexual union, and prefigures Paul D's vision of Sethe as a friend of his mind and his desire to place 'his story next to hers' (p. 273).

the wrought-iron on her back the hard, ridged scars

pay dirt earth or ore that yields profit to a miner

earth-over the natural oven that Sixo has made

shirt waist blouse

salsify herb with purple flowers

butter wouldn't come the milk wouldn't turn to butter when churned

bristle hog's hair for making ink (and paintbrushes)

checkers a game of draughts

Redmen American Indians

SECTION 3 PAGES 28–42

Fragments of the story of Denver's birth are recounted. Sethe allows herself to contemplate a future with Paul D

Several layers of narrative, told by different characters and set in different times, begin with describing Denver and the 'sweet' and increasingly adult games that she plays by herself in a green bower of boxwood bushes. There, she remembers the events of an evening several years ago, when, after a similar game, involving cologne and nudity, she returned home and saw her mother being embraced by a white dress. She interprets this vision as a sign that the baby ghost has plans. The weather and the sight of Sethe make her remember the story of her own birth, which she loves to tell and to hear told. The narrative switches to Sethe's voice. As she tells the tale of her escape from Sweet Home, she remembers the language and dancing of her own people and the vague relationship that she had with her own mother. We are presented with the image of Sethe staggering through the woods, very pregnant with Denver, her feet so swollen and bruised that she could hardly walk. She lay down in the snow and was discovered by Amy Denver, a white girl. Amy was on her way to Boston to buy velvet. Sethe crawled into a lean-to for the night, and Amy massaged her feet. This section is recounted in the present tense. We return to a more recent past. After Denver has told Sethe about the kneeling dress, Sethe tells Denver about schoolteacher who came to Sweet Home after the death of Mr Garner.

There is a shift to the immediate present of the novel and the progress of the narrative. Paul D has changed 124 Bluestone Road and the lives of its inhabitants. The ghost has gone. Sethe wakes up next to Paul D after their first night together, and remembers Denver's vision of several years before. She wonders about the nature of the 'plans' the baby could have. Paul D sings as he mends the furniture he had broken the day before. He recalls his own past: the prison work he was forced to do in Alfred, Georgia, and the songs he and the other men sang as they worked. He asks Sethe's permission to stay with her and Denver. Sethe is positive, and tells him not to worry about Denver's reaction since she is a charmed child. She tells him of Denver's miraculous birth and attributes Amy's appearance to Denver's destiny. After schoolteacher came to find them, and Sethe went to prison, Denver was not touched by the rats there although they ate everything else.

> Although Sethe and Amy are close in age and social standing (see Characterisation: Amy) the divisions that race imposes are immediate. Amy instinctively uses the terms of social denigration, calling Sethe 'nigger' and asking her if she is going to 'just lay there and foal?' (pp. 33–4) while Sethe calls her 'Miss' and is sufficiently suspicious to give a false name. However, the word 'yard-chat' (p. 33) signifies the partial dissolution of these boundaries. In the slow telling of this story, Amy operates in the roles of nurse, friend and midwife, although when she takes her leave of Sethe, she reverts to her position as 'Miss Amy Denver' (p. 85).

> Sethe realises that her home is without colour and that she has not missed it (p. 39). When Beloved is in the flesh and Sethe finally recognises her as her daughter, she is determined to notice colours and plants a garden out of season (p. 201). Denver would give up

colour for Beloved, so great is her love for her sister (p. 121). Baby
Suggs dedicates her last years to the contemplation of colour – as
she explains to Stamp (p. 179), something that does not hurt
anyone. The red blood and pink gravestone are the last colours that
Sethe remembers. Red is the colour that splashes the narrative,
whether it is Stamp Paid's red ribbon, or the cardinal bird seen by
Beloved.

Here, Sethe explains her vision of time. 'Some things go … some
things just stay' (p. 35). Her 'rememory' is what selects and
privileges certain events, and does not allow her to forget them.
Sethe believes that acts and actions remain. This is paralleled
in the novel by the author's own treatment of time, encoded
in the many layers of past experience and memories presented
in each section. When Sethe goes to the Clearing we live out
the experience of one of Baby Suggs's meetings (p. 87), and
when the women go to 124 they see themselves there as children
(p. 258). This is in contrast to **linear narrative** or chronological
history, where past events are fixed and incontrovertible. The
fluidity can be construed as a gendered and racial revision of
the way in which we tackle literature and history. The lack of
boundaries between time, experiences and subjects is echoed by
the condensed nature of the novel's **metaphors**, references and
language.

wild veronica the wild Speedwell, with bright blue flowers
the War Years the American Civil War (1861–5)
bloody side of the Ohio river the Ohio separates the state of Ohio from West
Virginia and Kentucky. Virginia was one of the eleven states that seceded
from the Federal Government. Kentucky was a slave state. Its governors
favoured secession but were defeated. Ohio shared northern liberal attitudes
and was urbanised rather than agricultural, as can be seen from Garner's
ecstatic praise of Cincinnati's civic development (p. 142). With the
Northwest Ordinance of 1787 slavery was prohibited in all territory north of
Ohio
mossy teeth teeth that are green through lack of cleaning
trash white trash, i.e. poor whites
pot liquor liquid left in the pot after cooking meat and/or vegetables

pay for ... passage this telling detail would suggest that Amy's mother was an immigrant. She too is heading for the freedom of the north, although Boston is much further away than she thinks

foal give birth like a mare

swole swollen

Lisle smooth cotton, usually used for hosiery and underwear

rememory a word combining memory, remembrance and the idea of repetition

emerald closet the enclosure of boxwood

serge worsted or wool, a practical, robust material

molly apple fruits from the American Molle tree, from which wine can be made

SECTION 4 PAGES 43–9

Denver insults Paul D and Sethe defends her daughter. Paul D, Sethe and Denver go to the carnival

Denver is less than happy about the relationship between her mother and Paul D. After three days she asks Paul D how long he intends to 'hang around'. Sethe is embarrassed, while Paul D is wounded. He drops the mug of coffee he is holding and asks if he should leave. Sethe says no and Denver once again is banished from the kitchen. Sethe and Paul D discuss the situation. Sethe apologises for her daughter's behaviour but will not permit Paul D to criticise her. Paul D thinks that Sethe loves too intensely. He tells her that it does not have to be a choice between Denver and himself, and offers his support if she wants to go 'inside' and tackle her buried memories.

At Paul D's suggestion, they decide to go to the carnival. It is Sethe's first outing in eighteen years. Their three shadows appear to be continually holding hands, independent of their actions. Denver is sullen while Paul D is in an infectiously good mood; smiling and talking to everyone who passes. The amusement of the carnival lies in seeing white people making fools of themselves. Denver feels more favourable towards Paul D, and on the way home their shadows are holding hands once again.

Sethe later identifies the hand-holding shadows as another Trinity composed of Denver, Sethe and the reincarnated Beloved (p. 182).

Paul D suggests to Sethe that they can have 'A life' together. This solitary noun is repeated three times on pages 46–7. Sethe is later to see her life as structured in eighteen-year periods of 'unlivable life', interrupted by moments of 'short-lived glory' (p. 173).

croaker sack bag made out of heavy cloth, such as burlap

sawyer someone who saws wood for a living

barker a person who proclaims the attractions and whets the interest of the crowd

Pickaninnies (derogatory) black children

horehound minty-tasting herb

SECTION 5 PAGES 50–6

A young woman calling herself Beloved is waiting for them outside 124. Denver takes charge of nursing her. The rift between Paul D and Denver deepens

A young black woman is waiting for them on a tree stump in front of 124 Bluestone Road when Paul D, Sethe and Denver return from the carnival. She has emerged from the river, and sleeps by the riverside for a day until she finds the strength to walk to 124. Her skin is soft and unlined and she is dressed in expensive clothes. As soon as Sethe sees her face she has to run to the outdoor privy, and, before reaching it, she is forced to urinate outside. The flow reminds her of when her waters broke at Denver's birth. The girl calls herself Beloved. She drinks four cupfuls of water and falls asleep. Denver is fascinated by the new guest. Paul D and Sethe do not press her for the details of her origins. Beloved sleeps for four days, nursed by Denver who is as patient with the invalid as she is irritable with her mother. Her behaviour makes Sethe realise how lonely Denver has been. Denver lies to her mother to protect Beloved, denying that the supposedly sick girl lifted the rocking chair with one hand. Paul D knows that she is lying, and 'if there had been an open latch between them, it had closed'.

There are lots of clues in the narrative that lead the reader to assume that the girl Beloved is the ghost come to life: the absence of Here Boy, the girl's new skin and unused shoes, the link that Sethe makes between her 'emergency' and her waters breaking, or the hairline scratches on Beloved's forehead. Sethe only realises who Beloved is in the first section of Two (p. 175) and only later vocalises the connections (pp. 202–3). She has to learn to reread her own narrative and the signs that her own body gives her. In Section 9 (pp. 86–105) she thinks that Denver and Beloved are like sisters but refuses to accept the implications of this thought.

Beloved is portrayed as a child. She is heavy-headed and slow-moving and has undeveloped motor skills. We later learn that she cannot tie her own shoe-laces (p. 65). Her greed for sugar prefigures her hunger for Sethe's presence and her stories. Beloved's gaze is also described in terms of hunger. Denver is 'licked, tasted, eaten' (p. 57). (See also Characterisation, on Beloved; Recurring Themes and Imagery, on Eating and Hunger.)

sorghum a cereal crop
'talking sheets' scandalous leaflets and newspapers
bluing a preparation of blue and violet dyes used to offset the discolouring of white sheets
taffy like toffee
lumbar the lumbar region is located in the lower back

SECTION 6 PAGES 57–63

Beloved asks Sethe questions about her past

Beloved is obsessed with Sethe and waits for her to get up in the morning and to come home from work at night. A month has passed since Beloved's arrival. She derives immense satisfaction from hearing about Sethe's past, and asks her questions that provoke stories. She asks Sethe about the earrings she once wore and Sethe tells the two girls about her wedding with Halle, enlarging upon the details provided in Section 2 (pp. 20–7). She stole pieces of fabric from which to sew a dress, that later she had to unpiece in order to return them to where she had originally found them. She had wanted some sort of celebration and Mrs Garner, recognising her desires, gave her a pair of crystal earrings as a present. Beloved asks Sethe whether her mother ever braided her hair. Sethe remembers that her mother and the other women spoke another language. She hardly knew her mother, who slept in a different cabin and was at work all day. The woman who nursed her was called Nan. She remembers Nan telling her that she was the only child that her mother claimed as her own. When they were on the boat travelling from Africa to America, Sethe's mother had various unwanted children whom she 'threw away' and did not name. Sethe remembers her mother showing her a branded mark on her ribcage by which she could always recognise her. We learn that Sethe's mother was hanged along with many of the other women on the farm, but that Sethe never found out for what reason. The section finishes with the question that is perplexing Denver. How could Beloved know to ask Sethe about her earrings?

> Thanks to Beloved's question about the earrings we learn more about Sethe's 'wedding' with Halle. Paul D remembered her bedding dress in Section 1 (p. 10), and at the end of Section 2, Sethe remembers telling Mrs Garner and being disappointed that there was to be no ceremony. The differing implications of the changed consonant – bedding/wedding – should be noticed. The eroticised corn scene is mentioned again here from a more distanced viewpoint, and is referred to as a honeymoon. The earrings are **symbolic** of the illusory freedom that existed at Sweet Home, destroyed with the arrival of schoolteacher. Sethe cites them as something that 'made her believe she could discriminate' (p. 188) in her last phase of utter disillusionment with whitefolks. The earrings are also mentioned in Section 9, when Sethe dangles them for the pleasure of the 'crawling already? girl' (p. 94). They were taken by the jailer in order to protect Sethe from damaging herself (p. 183). They also recur in Beloved's **asyntactic** monologue (p. 212).

> The relationship between Sethe and her mother is significant in terms of the novel's central complex analysis of maternal love. We learn that Sethe was only nursed for a few weeks. The fact that she has been dispossessed of her due rankles: 'There was no nursing milk to call my own' (p. 200) and 'another woman's tit that never had enough for all' (p. 203). Black women were often wet-nurses for the children of their white owners, another example of the appropriation of black bodies. This is part of the implications of schoolteacher's nephews' theft of Sethe's milk.

Milk comes to be a symbol of love, and its abundance is used throughout, 'milk enough for all' (pp. 16, 100), to show Sethe's power. Sethe remembers very little of her origins. She remembers the antelope dance (p. 31) and is haunted by the suspicion that she used to speak another language. This brings home the fact that the system of slavery denied roots and the access to one's history. Sethe does not know why her mother was hanged just as Baby Suggs does not know what happened to most of her children. Sethe is stripped of her bearings in what may be part of a conscious 'disremembering'. She asks Beloved: 'You disremember everything? I never knew my mother neither' (p. 119), making a subconscious association between active forgetting and the relationship between mothers and daughters.

Sethe only recognises her mother by her cloth hat and the mark on her chest. Sethe's childish request for a mark of her own is a desperate plea for a recognisable, if external, bond that would link the two of them. In the penultimate section of the novel Sethe complains that 'her ma'am had hurt her feelings and she couldn't find her hat anywhere' (p. 272). The fact that Sethe's mother claimed and named her is relevant. In relating the fact that Sethe's mother rejected, 'threw away' (p. 63), her unwanted offspring, the text centres the issue of infanticide. Ella also refused to nurse the result of her rape.

damper part of a stove that, when regulated, allows the passage of more or less air to the fire
zealot someone fanatical and enthusiastic
rutabaga large yellow root vegetable, like a turnip
peck a measure of capacity used for dry goods, equivalent to about two gallons
sweet william garden flower with large, colourful rosettes
press cupboard for clothes
dresser scarf runner for the dressing table

SECTION 7 PAGES 64–73

Beloved has been at 124 for five weeks. Paul D quizzes her, and she has a choking fit. Paul D tells Sethe that Halle had witnessed schoolteacher's nephews stealing her milk

Another week has passed. Beloved does not speak to Paul D. He perceives her as 'shining' with sexual readiness. After a meal he interrogates her about her family and origins. She seems to be different from the other persecuted black people he has known. He wants her to leave, and just as he is thinking of finding her a place to work in town, Beloved is seized by a choking fit. She and Denver retire, and from then on they sleep in the same room. Denver is very happy with this arrangement. Sethe is remonstrating with Paul D and reminds him of the dangers that beset homeless black women. The subject of Halle comes up, and Sethe reveals her bitterness at his failure to meet up with her in order to escape together. Paul D tells her that Halle was in the loft and witnessed her rape by schoolteacher's nephews. The last time that Paul D saw Halle he was sitting by the butter churn with butter all over his face. This is the piece of information which he had decided that she need never know in Section 1. Paul D saw Halle but couldn't speak to him because he had a bit in his mouth. He is the last of the Sweet Home men: 'one crazy, one sold, one missing, one burnt'. He tells Sethe how the sight of a rooster named Mister brought home his own impotence. He realised that it had more identity and freedom than he did although he was a man and the other a bird. Schoolteacher had changed Paul D irrevocably.

> The conversation between Sethe and Paul D is arranged like a piece of music. Their questions and answers, repeated in their entirety, or varied only by a pronoun or a negative, form a counterpoint. The repetitions of 'Slowly, slowly' and 'carefully, carefully' are in contrast to Sethe's frantic questioning, 'He saw? He saw? He saw?'.

> Beloved's language is limited and simplistic, her vocabulary undeveloped, reflecting her infantile nature.

diddled played with

regulators bands of volunteer committees in the USA who saw their role as to preserve order, prevent crime and administer justice. All too often this justice involved violence and racism

paterollers patrollers

posses gangs of white men who roam at night, administering their own brand of justice

Klan Ku Klux Klan (KKK). A secret organisation originating in southern USA after the Civil War that aimed to maintain white supremacy by violent means

dragon one of the titles that is awarded to leaders within the KKK is 'Grand Dragon'

clabber sour milk that has thickened or curdled

peeps chicks

SECTION 8 PAGES 74–85

Beloved and Denver dance. Denver tells the story of her birth

Beloved dances with Denver. She tells Denver about the place where she was before she came to 124 Bluestone Road. It was hot and full of dead people. She claims that she came back to see Sethe, and remembers playing with Denver in her bower. Denver wants Beloved to promise not to tell Sethe who she really is. In order to appease her she tells the story of her birth, beginning from where the narrative left off in Section 3. She tells of Amy and her quest for velvet and the way she massaged Sethe's feet. Denver feels that the events of the story are happening to her and Sethe's voice takes over the narrative. It was Amy who described the wounds of Sethe's bleeding back as a tree. She dressed Sethe's ravaged back with spider webs and sang to her. She forbade Sethe to die in the night and they settled down to sleep. Amy padded Sethe's misshapen feet with leaves. They arrived at the Ohio river and found a broken boat. Sethe's waters broke and she gave birth to Denver on the banks of the Ohio. Amy helped and together they wrapped the new-born baby in their underwear. Sethe agreed to give it the name of her protector, and Denver is 'christened'.

The text reflects the movements of the dancing gi[l]
prose is musical: 'A little two-step, two-step, m[
slide, slide and strut on down.' The repetitions and
echo their movements: 'round and round ... to and fro, to and fro'
(p. 74). The sense of play extends to the language and the pun
describing the 'catching' laughter 'caught', immediately suggests the
image of a game.

Here the story of Denver's birth continues to evolve. It began in
Section 1, with the reference to the white girl who helped Sethe and
the tree on Sethe's back. In Section 3 the story develops and we
learn more of Sethe's encounter with Amy and get as far as the
massaging of Sethe's feet. In Section 5 the boat and Sethe's
breaking waters are mentioned and this is where the narrative picks
up. In the telling of this tale, memories merge: 'Denver was seeing
it now and feeling it – through Beloved. Feeling how it must have
felt to her mother' (p. 78). The story continues in Section 9.

mossy teeth on this occasion, means the two nephews of schoolteacher. An
example of **synecdoche**
tail the end of a gust of wind
hankering can mean strong desire, yearning. Here suggests leaning over

SECTION 9 PAGES 86–105

**Sethe goes to the Clearing where invisible fingers around
her neck try to choke her. She remembers her arrival at
124 and Denver's school-going days and subsequent two
years of deafness**

Sethe misses Baby Suggs and her calming presence. To pay homage to
Halle, whom she now knows must be dead, and to the stirred-up
memories of her past, she decides to go to the Clearing, accompanied by
the two girls. She describes the way 124 Bluestone Road was as she first
knew it, during her twenty-eight days of nonenslaved life. It was a
meeting place, and a place in which people congregated and received
messages. Baby Suggs was an unchurched preacher before she took to her
bed. Her sermons took place in the Clearing and evoked self-love and
respect amongst the members of her black congregation.

There is a flashback to Sethe's past. She remembers waking up on the banks of the Ohio, after giving birth to Denver. Amy had gone. Stamp Paid helped her to cross the river, where she was met by a woman called Ella. When she arrived for the first time at 124 Bluestone Road, Baby Suggs washed her, treated her wounded back and feet, uncaking the dried milk from her nipples and binding her womb. The next day she was reunited with her three children whom she had sent ahead. The baby girl played with her crystal earrings.

The narrative returns to the present tense. Sethe is in the Clearing with the girls. She asks the spirit of Baby Suggs to massage her neck. At first it obliges, gentle and reassuring, but then the ghostly fingers begin to choke her. Beloved and Denver run to her rescue, and Beloved touches and kisses Sethe's neck, behaving as if she were a baby. At first Sethe thinks that Baby Suggs has tried to kill her, but then she realises that the touch was not that of her mother-in-law. The touch resembled that of the spirit that used to inhabit 124 Bluestone Road and she concludes that it must have retreated to the Clearing after Paul D banished it from the house. For a moment she thinks that the ghostly fingers and Beloved's caresses are one and the same, but she puts the thought out of her mind. She realises that Denver and Beloved behave as if they are sisters, each compensating and fulfilling the needs of the other and showing no competitiveness in their affection to her.

When they get home, Paul D embraces Sethe. We learn that Beloved is jealous of Paul D and of the time that Sethe spends with him. Denver accuses Beloved of being the one to choke her mother. Denver is convinced that Beloved is her sister come back to life. She remembers when she was seven and spent a year going to school at Lady Jones's until a fellow schoolboy, Nelson Lord, asked her whether it was true that Sethe had murdered her baby sister. When she reported this conversation to her mother she went deaf rather than hear Sethe's answer. She stopped attending the school, and lived in a world cut off from sound for two years. The first thing that she heard was the baby ghost trying to climb the stairs. From that point on the baby was characterised by its spiteful behaviour, the venomous presence that the two women attempt to summon and that is described in the first sentence of the book. Denver has always been the most sensitive and most needful of the ghost's presence, since it was her companion when she was a child. She feels that

Beloved is hers and realises that she is prepared to betray Se
behalf. Beloved watches turtles mating, and sees how the female will risk
everything for one touch of the male.

The physicality of Baby Suggs's call, using the model of call-and-
response prayer incites her audience to listen and love their bodies
(see Critical History, on Post-Modern Criticism).

Sethe goes to the clearing to 'listen to the spaces' (p. 89) just as Ella
listens for the 'holes' (p. 92) in Sethe's tale. Sethe describes the
'empty space' about Halle's fate (p. 95). *Beloved* is full of these gaps
underlining the impossibility of a totalised narrative. We do not
know whether Beloved really is Sethe's daughter or what she really
is. We do not learn what happened to Halle just as Sethe does not
know why her mother was hanged. This not knowing was one of
the results of slavery which, in its system of moving people around,
effectively destroyed the possibility of familial memory and the
correlative sense of identity.

The description of the mating turtles is erotic: an example of
Morrison's 'prose-poetry'. The five verbs create great density of
meaning. The **assonance** of 'placed plates' and the **onomatopaeia**
of clashing and 'pat pat pat' augment the physicality of the
scene. When Beloved seduces Paul D she is compared to the turtles
(p. 116).

AME African Methodist Episcopal, an offshoot of Methodism founded in
1787 by Richard Allen, a former slave. In the 1840s there were many
female converts to this religion, particularly in Ohio. Women such as Jarena
Lee and Julia Foote challenged male-dominated mid-century Methodism by
preaching and travelling without official recognition

leavins left-overs

slop for hogs used as food for the pigs

flatbed flatboat or flat-bottomed boat

cardinal bird with a red crest

four o'clocks plant whose flowers need sunlight and only open late in the
afternoon

SECTION 10 PAGES 106–13

Paul D's experience in the chain gang

Paul D tells us in the present tense of his experiences in the prison camp in Alfred, Georgia. He was sent there after he attempted to kill Brandywine, the man to whom schoolteacher sold him after the break-up of Sweet Home. He was one of forty-six men who worked in a chain gang. They lived in wooden boxes set in a ditch. In the morning each man was linked to the others by a length of chain, and the white guards selected men at random to perform fellatio on them. During the day the men worked together, singing as they swung their sledge hammers. Paul D had been there for eighty-six days when it began to rain and after nine days of downpour they were compelled to stop working. They were left chained up inside their boxes. It rained so hard that the mud roofs began to cave in. The men escaped by diving underneath the iron bars that formed one side of their boxes. The fact that they were all linked by the chain meant that each and every one was brought to salvation. They found themselves with an exiled and sick band of Cherokee Indians, who fed them and helped them remove the chains. Paul D asked their advice as to how he could get to the North and they told him to follow the blossom on the trees. He followed their advice, and on the way he spent a year and a half in Delaware with a 'weaver lady'.

> The men learn alternative ways of speaking. They read each other's eyes, speak to each other through songs and communicate via the chain itself, thus transforming what imprisons them into a vehicle for communication (see Critical History, on Post-Modern Criticism).

> In this section Morrison gives a brief insight into the sufferings of the Cherokee Indians. There is a reference to another tribe in Section 17 (p. 155). The Native Americans, like the African slaves, were dispossessed of their language and rights.

> **buckboard** open carriage
> **coffle** a group of slaves chained together for travelling
> **feldspar** any aluminium silicate. Can be flesh-red, bluish or greenish. Here it refers to a feldspar quarry

bay to cry or shout. The word has bestial associations

cottonmouths a venomous water snake that flourishes in ditches, called so because of the white interior of its mouth

unshriven dead someone who has not been given absolution before death

redbud trees Judas trees; bushy trees with pink or red flowers

Cherokee a tribe of native Americans who originally numbered 45,000 and possessed large tracts of land. They sided with the English in most disputes between European colonists and with the Royalist party in the Revolutionary War. With the increasing number of white settlers they were dispossessed of most of their land

for whom a rose was named the Cherokee rose (*rosa laevigata*) is a climbing rose with fragrant white blossom

Oklahoma those who had not moved were driven to the northeastern corner of Oklahoma

George III (1738–1820) King of England 1760–1811, during Britain's War of Independence with the USA

published as a newspaper Elias Boudinot edited *The Cherokee Phoenix* (1828–35), the first newspaper for an Indian tribe

Oglethorpe (1697–1785) the founder of the state of Georgia

Andrew Jackson (1767–1845) the seventh president of the USA. When America and Great Britain went to war in 1812 the Creek Indians staged their own attack on the Americans, Jackson was the general in charge of the Tennessee troops

wrote their language the Cherokee written alphabet of eighty-five characters was invented in 1821 by George Guess; also known as Sequoyah

barnacles pincers placed in a horse's nostrils to prevent it moving while being shod

Free North the Northern States opposed the Confederate States on many issues. One of these was slavery

SECTION **11** PAGES 114–17

Beloved moves Paul D out of Sethe's bed and into the cold house. She appears to him one night and they have sex

Paul D stops sleeping with Sethe at night. At first he sleeps in the rocking chair, then in Baby Suggs's room, then in the storeroom and finally in the cold house. He realises that it is not through any discontent on his own part but that he is being moved by someone else, who has prevented him from being with Sethe. One night Beloved comes to visit him in the coldroom. She lifts her skirts and asks him to touch her 'on the inside part'. He remonstrates with her, reminding her of how much Sethe loves her, but Beloved persists in her desire to be touched and called by name. Finally Paul D succumbs and finds himself saying, over and over again 'Red heart. Red heart. Red heart.'

> Beloved demands that Paul D: 'Call me my name'. The issues of calling and naming, present in the novel from the bible quotation in the preliminary pages, are vital to *Beloved*. The section comes to a close with Paul D crying out the words 'Red heart' as the tobacco tin that is his heart falls apart. In the novel, the heart is **symbolic** of the ability to love. Baby Suggs dedicates herself to her heart. She notices its beating only when she has been freed, and it collapses after Sethe's action in the woodshed. Paul D has locked up his feelings in a tin box. This image of enclosure in metal can only suggest slavery. It is one of several images of boxes and closure. In the epilogue the 'latch latched' (p. 275) refers to the repression of the memories of Beloved. Similarly the closure of a potential relationship between Paul D and Denver is described as a literal closing: 'if there had been an open latch between them, it would have closed' (p. 56). Sethe describes her discovery of Beloved as 'a hobnail casket of jewels' (p. 176) which must be opened with care.

Lot's wife Lot's wife was turned to a pillar of salt when she looked back as she and her husband fled from Sodom (Genesis 19:1–26)

SECTION 12 PAGES 118–24

Beloved disappears and frightens Denver

Denver is convinced that Beloved is her sister. She is very careful not to press her for information, for fear that Beloved might leave and she be left alone once more. Sethe questions Beloved about her background and her clothing, and confesses her suspicions to Denver. Denver refrains from agreeing with her mother. She loves being looked at by Beloved, and thinks of tasks and ways in which they might be prolonged in order to occupy the mysterious guest. One day the two girls go into the cold house in order to get the cider jug. Beloved disappears. Denver is desperate. Her source of life has disappeared. After some time Beloved comes back. She explains to Denver that she does not want to return to the other place: 'This is the place I am.'

> For an examination of the food **metaphors** see Recurring Themes and Imagery, on Eating and Hunger. The passage describing Beloved's disappearance is written in the immediate present: 'This day they are outside', indicating a continuity of the days filled with tasks, listed in a series of incomplete **paratactic** phrases in the previous paragraph. It also gives a sense of immediacy to Denver's panic, since the events are not recounted with the assurance of retrospect.

shoot an exclamation of surprise or annoyance

SECTION 13   PAGES 125–32

Paul D makes up his mind to tell Sethe about his relationship with Beloved but instead he asks her if she will give him a child

Paul D feels that he is being forced into having sex with Beloved. His powerlessness makes him question his manhood. When he was at Sweet Home, Mr Garner prided himself that Paul D and the other slaves were men. Now Paul D wonders whether he is a man, or whether it was only a definition. He decides to tell Sethe in the hope that she will help him. He goes to meet her after work, and instead of admitting his weakness, he finds himself asking her if she will have his child. It seems the solution to his problems. She laughs, and says she is too old. It starts snowing and Paul D carries Sethe on his back. They are happy and so absorbed in each other that they are surprised to see Beloved who has come to meet Sethe. The perfect moment is interrupted. That evening Sethe invites Paul D to sleep in her room, undoing Beloved's power to make him sleep in the cold house. Paul D remembers the last time he had been grateful to a woman. When he arrived in Delaware the weaver-lady gave him a meal and a bed to sleep in for the first time in his life. Sethe lies next to him and thinks that he is jealous of her existing daughters, and that is why he wants to have his own child. She too, like Denver, is beginning to think of Beloved as the baby girl come back to life.

'They were a family somehow and he was not the head of it.' In her novels, Morrison revises the definition of family (see Recurring Themes and Imagery, on Community and Family). Halle redefines his role as husband and becomes more like a brother (p. 25). Here, Sethe is beginning to realise the identity of Beloved. She refers to her peeing outside as 'broke water'. She also defines what motherhood means to her: 'to be good enough, alert enough, strong enough, *that* caring again'.

Paul D thinks of a child he might father with Sethe as a 'document' of his manhood, and she also perceives a child as a 'sign'. These nouns signal procreation as another way of 'writing' history. One could apply this **metaphor** to the system of slavery which, in denying parents their right to their children, parallels the similar denial of history and roots, not to mention the physical act of writing. Teaching slaves to read and write was prohibited and punished in many Southern states. Morrison is reviving this history, as she did in non-fiction form in the *Black Book*.

Paul D defines his sense of impotence by using three evocative animal metaphors. He lists a series of powerless, sexually inadequate and mute beasts, lacking teeth, horns and penises, in order to convey how schoolteacher made him feel.

steer bulls bulls castrated before sexual maturity

shucking corn husks

cobs small stacks of grain or hay

SECTION 14 PAGES 133–4

Beloved loses a tooth

Denver warns Beloved that Sethe might object if she causes Paul D to go away. Beloved is not listening and pulls a wisdom tooth out of her mouth. She thinks that it is only a matter of time before she explodes into her various components. She cries in the kitchen, holding the tooth in her hand. It is snowing outside.

This is one of the rare moments in which we eavesdrop on Beloved's thoughts in the first person. Her words are more often given in the form of reported speech.

SECTION 15 PAGES 135–47

The story of the feast at 124 which took place shortly after Sethe's arrival. Baby Suggs remembers her trip to Cincinnati with Mr Garner and the arrangements made for her as a free person

Stamp Paid had picked two bucketsful of blackberries and brought them to 124 Bluestone Road. Baby Suggs decided to make some pies, and to invite a few neighbours. The project for the feast grew and grew, and that evening the house hosted and fed almost ninety people. Next day Baby Suggs sensed disapproval in the air. She was in the garden while Stamp Paid chopped wood. She realised that she had exaggerated, breaking her own rule of 'Good is knowing when to stop' (p. 87). Her display of bounty had irritated their guests. Behind the smell of disapproval and envy she discerned something else, 'dark and coming'. As she wondered what it could be, we learn about her life at Sweet Home. She was bought by Mr Garner with her ten-year-old son Halle. She cost relatively little because she had a broken hip. Sweet Home was small compared to other places she had been, and her job consisted of assisting Mrs Garner with the household chores. Her hip caused her pain, and, after ten years, Halle decided to pay for her freedom with his own labour. At first she agreed only to make him happy, but when she arrived in Cincinnati with Mr Garner she realised that there was 'nothing like freedom in the world'. She noticed her hands and felt her heart beating for the first time. Jenny had been the name on her bill-of-sale, but she decided to keep the name of Baby Suggs, in the hope that she would be found by the man she had claimed as husband, and who had given her the name of Baby and his name, Suggs. They went to visit Garner's friends, the Bodwins. The sister and brother were both against slavery. They found a house for Baby and suggested that she could do washing and mend shoes for a living. Baby Suggs had imagined that she might be able to reunite her family. Of her eight children, she knew that two were dead, but hoped to be able to contact four of the others. After two years she realised that it was impossible. She contented herself with Halle, and the news that he was married and that Sethe was pregnant.

During this reminiscence, Baby Suggs had remained immobile in the garden. She regretted the munificence of the feast. She felt the disapproval of her neighbours and saw the image of a pair of high-topped shoes.

> This section focuses on two past scenes, one in the present tense (the continuing story of Sethe's drastic act which has been in the telling since the first section of the book) and the other, the tale of Baby Suggs's arrival, placed as a memory within the other narrative.
>
> We see the relevance of freedom for Baby Suggs who, as a slave, was not able to know herself in any sense, denied of the 'map' to discover what she was like (p. 140). After her own hands, she recognises her own heart beating, that later through her preaching will be rechannelled into her community. This self-ownership chronicles a transition from being objectified property to being a subject. As Sethe comments: 'Freeing yourself was one thing; claiming ownership of that freed self was another' (p. 95). Sethe, too, experiences freedom to love when she arrives at Sweet Home (p. 162). Denver's feeling that she does not exist without Beloved and that her own self has disappeared is another kind of slavery (p. 123).
>
> The **polyphonic** narrative gives voice to the community's outrage at Baby Suggs's abundance. Morrison uses italic to emphasise the irritation at Suggs's ostentatious miracle. The biblical reference is no accident: 'Loaves and fishes were His powers' (p. 137). Baby Suggs works an act of magic, making a feast for ninety people with almost magical ingredients: vegetables out of season and fresh cream 'but no cow'.

hominy boiled kernels of dried sweetcorn
gone to Glory died
Bishop Allen Richard Allen was the first bishop of the AME church

Schoolteacher arrives at 124 to take back Sethe and her children. Sethe has taken them all to the woodshed and tried to kill them. She is arrested and leaves with Denver in her arms

Schoolteacher, with one of his nephews, the sheriff and a slave catcher drove up to 124 Bluestone Road to take back Sethe and her children in order to restock Sweet Home. They found Stamp Paid and Baby Suggs in the garden. Sethe was in the woodshed. She had cut her toddler's throat with a handsaw and had attempted to do the same to Howard and Buglar. She was in the process of trying to smash three-week-old Denver's head against the wall planks. For a moment we hear schoolteacher's thoughts. He refers to Sethe as if she were an animal, gone wild because of having been overbeaten. He regarded this as a pity since she has ten breeding years left. schoolteacher's nephew was shaking, unable to understand why Sethe had committed such an awful act.

Baby Suggs came into the woodshed and immediately nursed Howard and Buglar. Sethe would not relinquish her dead toddler. Baby Suggs told her to feed Denver, and insisted that she hold only one baby at a time. Sethe fed Denver with a nipple covered with the blood of her sister. Sethe and Denver were taken away in a cart. A crowd of neighbours was there to watch, and they hummed as she left. Baby Suggs was wishing that she had kept Denver, when two white children came and brought her a pair of high-topped shoes to mend.

This section falls into two parts. The first is recounted from the slave-catchers' point of view. Morrison's omniscience allows us to enter the sheriff, schoolteacher and the nephew's psyches. This choice of narrator for the central event of the novel has various implications. It distances the reader from the drama of the events, thus increasing the horrific aspect of the passage, while simultaneously validating Sethe's response to the system that schoolteacher represents. The sustained use of animal imagery, schoolteacher's view of blacks as 'creatures', like farm animals, and the sheriff's opinion that black people are cannibals help the reader to understand what Sethe is seeking to protect her children from.

The repetition of 'nigger ... eyes' in the description of the carnage is chilling. Recognising Baby Suggs as the crazy 'woman with a flower in her hat' gives the reader a jolt. The careful description of her uprooting the rue comes from the previous section (p. 138). Here there is a bitter **irony** since rue also means sorrow, pity, regret. Ophelia in *Hamlet* (IV.5) hands out rue, and Shakespeare plays on this double meaning.

Schoolteacher has come to 'claim' his property. This is a verb which is also used to describe the act of self-assertion. In the epilogue Beloved is described: 'Although she has claim, she is not claimed' (p. 276). Like the acts of naming and calling, claiming is another example words having different resonance according to the context in which they are used and, in this novel, the race of the user (see Recurring Themes and Imagery, on Naming).

In the second section (beginning on p. 151), there is a change of perspective and we witness Baby Suggs taking control, and the verification of her presentiment.

coons (derogatory) black people

SECTION **17** PAGES 154–8

Stamp Paid shows Paul D the newspaper cutting about Sethe. Paul D refuses to accept that it is her image

Stamp Paid takes Paul D aside and shows him a newspaper cutting about Sethe. Paul D cannot read, but gazes at the picture, and tells Stamp that it cannot be Sethe because the mouth is drawn wrongly. He looks at the picture with a sense of trepidation. Black people rarely appeared in newspapers unless involved in some kind of crime or atrocity. Stamp tries to explain the events that have just been told in the last section. He describes the difficulty of procuring the blackberries, and explains why he and Baby had been looking in the wrong direction the following day. He believes that nobody warned them of the approach of the white men, with the 'righteous look' because they were disgruntled after the excesses of the feast the night before. Paul D keeps interrupting him to say that the picture is not of Sethe. Stamp gives up on his own account of events, and reads the newspaper article to Paul D. Paul D still does not believe it can have been Sethe.

The narrative returns to the present of the novel. Stamp Paid tells his version of the Sethe's behaviour, which begins with his hard-won harvest of blackberries, and in this way, adds his voice to the collage of voices. This is another illustration of the **dialogic** nature of Morrison's narrative style. He retells from his point of view what Baby Suggs has already recounted in Section 15 and what Sethe will try to explain to Paul D in Section 18.

SECTION 18 PAGES 159–65

Paul D shows Sethe the newspaper excerpt. Sethe attempts to explain her actions. He rebukes her and leaves 124

Paul D has shown Sethe the newspaper clipping, hoping that the two of them will be able to laugh at the mix-up and at Stamp's interference. Sethe tries to tell him her account of events. She circles around the subject. She tells him how surprised she was to find the baby girl crawling already when she arrived at 124 Bluestone Road. She explains that, without female company or advice at Sweet Home, she was never quite sure how to look after her children. She tells him how proud she was to have escaped from Sweet Home on her own. Her stolen freedom brought with it the power to love. She realised that her children must never live the kind of life she had lived. When she recognised schoolteacher's hat she knew that she had to protect her children. By killing them she foiled schoolteacher's plans and she sent them to safety. Paul D is scared by the way Sethe explains her actions. As far as he is concerned her love is 'too thick'. He challenges her solution, and reminds her that, despite her efforts, Howard and Buglar are as good as lost, while Denver is timid and the baby girl is dead. He judges her, and tells her that she is a human being, and not a beast: 'You got two feet, Sethe, not four.' He does not say goodbye but takes his hat, and leaves, saying he will be back late.

Circling is repeated four times to describe Sethe's slow approach to her subject matter. Other **synonyms** are used: 'spinning', 'wheeled' 'turned' and Sethe is described as physically circling Paul D and the room, her body echoing her unconscious linguistic strategy. The phrase that describes this (p. 163) is an example of **zeugma**. Sethe's speech pattern is itself circular and Morrison's own narrative style throughout the novel demonstrates a similar circling, allowing images to prompt others and referring back and forward to events. Sethe thinks of herself as having been attacked by hummingbirds and uses the verb 'fly' to describe her movements. Stamp Paid has also described her as metamorphosing into a bird (p. 157).

sassafras dried, aromatic root bark from which antiseptic oil is obtained
Comfrey herb with soothing properties
through the veil see W.E.B. DuBois's use of the **metaphor** of the veil in 'On the Passing of the First Born', which describes his son's escape from segregation through death. Morrison herself uses the concept of a veil in 'The Site of Memory'. She has to 'rip the veil' behind which the slave narrator was forced to hide, and 'part the veil' that was normally drawn
heft weight, substance

Two

SECTION **1** PAGES 169–99

Stamp Paid determines to knock on Sethe's door. He regrets having shown Paul D the newspaper clipping. Sethe and the girls go ice-skating. Sethe realises who Beloved is. Stamp Paid remembers Baby Suggs. He quarrels with Ella when he learns that Paul D has moved out and is sleeping in the church. Sethe is late for work. Memories of Sweet Home are related

A year has passed since the time in which the novel began. 124 Bluestone Road is resounding with the voices of black women. Stamp Paid goes to the front door. He wants to apologise to Sethe for the lack of consideration he has shown her as Baby Suggs's 'kin'. He regrets his readiness to show Paul D the newspaper clipping. He has since realised that he may have denied Sethe her chance of happiness, and Denver the presence of a normal man in her home. The last time he visited the house was on the occasion of Baby Suggs's funeral. The neighbours attended out of respect for the dead woman, but refused to eat the food that Sethe had prepared. The necessary formality of Stamp Paid's visit prevents him from carrying out his intentions. He remembers his former anger towards Baby Suggs when she gave up her religious duties and devoted the remainder of her life to the contemplation of colour. Now he begins to understand why she lost her faith and her will to participate. He remembers a conversation that they had. She tells him that despite her belief in God and her freedom, the white men nevertheless intruded into her private familial space: 'they came in my yard'.

Sethe tries to forget the unpleasant turn her life has taken. She takes the two girls ice-skating. They fall and laugh, and come home to a change of clothes and hot sweet milk. They are sitting in front of the fire when Sethe realises that Beloved must be her daughter. Beloved is humming a song that Sethe invented and once sang to her children. Despite the implications of this knowledge Sethe remains calm, and leaves the girls to sleep in front of the fire. Next morning she cooks breakfast for the girls and is late for work. She now thinks that the shadows holding hands on the day of the carnival represented herself and her two daughters. She is full of hope that her sons too might return. She desires nothing other than what is in her house. She is excited by the idea that she will no longer have to explain or remember the events of the past. She makes a mental list of all the things that she can now forget and in the process she describes her stay in prison and her attendance at the baby's funeral.

When Stamp overcomes his pride, and knocks at the door of 124 Bluestone Road, Sethe is at work. He sees Beloved and Denver through the window. They do not respond to his knock. He goes to see Ella, the woman who met Sethe on the other side of the Ohio and took her to 124 for the first time. He asks her if she knows who the strange woman at the house could be. She does not know but tells him that Paul D is sleeping in the church cellar. He is astonished that the community of black people could let one of their number sleep in the cold without offering him a place in which to stay. Ella is wary of Paul D because of his association with Sethe. She has never been convinced that Sethe was Halle's wife, or that her children were really Baby Suggs's grandchildren. Stamp explains that Paul D and Sethe knew each other at Sweet Home, and that Paul D left Sethe after hearing about the murder she committed. It seems that this information changes Ella's attitude to Paul D.

At work Sethe ignores the reproaches of her employer. She is angry
with 'whitefolks' and no longer makes any distinction between those who
sought to help her, like the Bodwins or Amy, and those who perpetrate
the innumerable evils against black people. Her mind is flooded with
Sweet Home memories. The thought of Beloved at home makes her
conscious of all the things from which she has succeeded in saving her
children. She remembers schoolteacher measuring her with string, and
making two lists to compare her human and animal characteristics. She
thinks of her work on the farm, and her laughing sons and baby daughter.
She recalls the realisation that her sons too would have to work, and that
Halle, made to work full-time at Sweet Home, was denied the possibility
of purchasing freedom for himself or his family.

Here, Sethe moves from thinking of Beloved as 'Denver's friend'
(p. 173) to recognising her daughter fully. She initially associates
the shadows holding hands with Paul D (p. 173) but later sees
them as a **symbol** of her daughters and herself (p. 182). Sethe's
recognition of Beloved as her daughter creates a 'timeless present'
(p. 184), a 'no-time' (p. 191. Sethe is relieved of having to
remember: the presence of Beloved absolves her of some of the
weight of the past (see Structure, on Treatment of Time).
Returning from work, when Sethe sees her house, she thinks that it
is as if her baby daughter had never needed a headstone and as if her
heart had never stopped beating. This statement sends back a ripple
of references throughout the text. The pink headstone and Sethe's
payment are present in the first section of One, and referred to
subsequently (pp. 201, 204, 208, 241) while the mention of a
beating heart cannot but remind the reader of the chilling
description of Sethe feeling her daughter's heart stopping with
schoolteacher's every backwards step (p. 164). The hot milk that the
women drink after their ice-skating escapade joins the milk imagery
which informs the novel, and is linked with Sethe's claim of having
'milk enough for all' (p. 198) which is extended in the second
section of Two.

The dialogue between Stamp Paid and Ella is an example of
Morrison's skill at faithfully rendering the inherent incongruities of
speech. Incomplete phrases, rhetorical questions, exclamations

and double negatives abound. Their **metaphors**: 'Don't jump if you can't see the bottom' – 'I'm on dry land ... you the one wet' (pp. 186–7) enhance the immediacy of the passage.

Fugitive Bill a series of laws passed to protect the property rights of slave-owners, which imposed severe penalties on runaway slaves. The Fugitive Slave Act of 1793 was strengthened in 1850, and it is to this that Sethe refers

manumission formal emancipation from slavery

Dred Scott a slave who married and had two children while on free soil, but with his family was later taken back to Missouri. In 1846 he sued for his freedom. The Supreme Court there held that he was still a slave and had no standing in the court, whereas the USA Circuit Court decided that, while still a slave, he had standing as a citizen. The Supreme Court decided, however, that Scott was not a citizen. This ruling denied the rights of Congress to make slaves or their descendants citizens, and made it clear that slavery would not be abolished along constitutional lines

Sojourner's high-wheeled buggy Sojourner Truth (?1797–1883) was a female slave. Legally freed, her *Narrative*, transcribed by friends, was published in two versions in 1850 and 1875. She campaigned against tobacco, fashionable dress, alcohol and the segregation of street cars. She fought for evangelism, black people and women's rights

North Star an anti-slavery newspaper (1847–64) founded in Rochester, New York. It favoured peaceful political methods

bed life a life of sexual activity for Sethe

taters potatoes

head cheese the meat of the head, feet and sometimes of the tongue and heart of a pig cut up finely and seasoned and boiled. This mixture was made into a large sausage or pressed into a thin jellied mass

shoat a young pig of either sex

would a would have. Morrison is using colloquial speech to represent Sethe's frantic thought patterns

train this is a reference to the Underground Railroad, a secret network that existed before the Civil War. Fugitive slaves were given clothes and food and helped to escape. Harriet Tubman was one of the most famous black agents. It is significant that Morrison chooses to represent a female

conductor (pp. 198, 202) since by this action she commemorates the role
of women in the organisation of the Railroad
long-school people who have studied

SECTION 2 PAGES 200–4

Sethe's thoughts

Sethe's thoughts, unspeakable and unspoken, are conveyed in fragments.
She is proud that Beloved has come back to her. She justifies her
behaviour by remembering the horrors that would have awaited her
children at Sweet Home. She recalls her own relationship with her
mother, whom she scarcely saw, and her relationship with Mrs Garner,
whom she nursed. She plans her new life with her daughter back from the
dead. For the first time since the pink of the baby's gravestone she is
noticing colours, and she dwells on all the things she will be able to show
and explain to Beloved. She blames Paul D for obscuring the facts that
indicated Beloved's identity. Without his presence she is sure that she
would have noticed earlier the scratches on Beloved's forehead that
correspond to the marks of her fingernails and would have recognised the
implications of the way in which her waters seemed to break when she
was involuntarily forced to urinate on seeing her daughter. She thinks
that she would have questioned the way in which Beloved knew to ask
about the crystal earrings, or connected their physical similarities.

This section, and the two that follow it show the thoughts of the
three main female **protagonists** narrated in a vivid present tense,
using a technique known as '**stream of consciousness**' or **interior
monologue**.

Sethe's thoughts are presented with short staccato phrases (p. 202)
and many repetitions and affirmations. They are **associative**, and
skip and leap from subject to subject. Thinking of her daughter
makes Sethe remember her own mother (pp. 200, 203) and her
traumatic childhood and her sense of loss is reaffirmed: she was
denied her share of maternal milk and her mother was hanged. The
subject of motherhood prompts Sethe's subconscious definition of
the term: 'When I tell you you mine, I also mean I'm yours'
(p. 203). She cannot draw breath without her children and only

identifies herself as a mother. Memories of the stealing of her milk crop up (pp. 200, 202), adding yet more horror to the scene which has been developing since the first section of One, as do references to the headstone (pp. 201, 204).

holler shout

spigot tap

SECTION 3 PAGES 205–9

Denver's thoughts

Denver claims Beloved as her sister. Her memory of her loneliness as a child, her only company the ghost, is followed by a description of her fear of her mother. Howard and Buglar used to frighten her, and she lived with the apprehension that what made it appropriate for her mother to kill her own children might happen again. She used to dream that her mother decapitated her every night and feels that she has to protect Beloved from her mother. The half-hidden memories of the rats and the time she spent in prison return to her. She is convinced that Halle, her 'daddy' will return. She has spent her childhood waiting for him, and hoarding the stories that Baby Suggs used to recount about her favourite son. Denver dreams of being united with her father and of living with him and Beloved. Sethe is denied a place in this dream scenario.

> Sethe's thoughts are followed by a similar monologue from Denver. While Sethe's interior monologue is motivated by guilt and the need to explain, Denver's thoughts are full of her fears, dreams and loneliness

SECTION 4 PAGES 210–13

Beloved's thoughts

We see Beloved at the stage of primary identification with her mother: 'I am not separate from her'. Her viewpoint is infantile and incomplete, rather like Denver's partial memories of the jail (p. 206). Beloved also remembers the grape arbor that Sethe has described, but then goes on to recount the time she spent with the dead. She tells of what seems to be a sea-voyage. This can be read as the story of the slaves who came to

America from Africa: the mouldy bread, chains around people's necks, cramped conditions and segregation of the sexes. The entire passage is highly impressionistic but finishes by chronicling Beloved's birth into the world, recounted in One, Section 5.

> This section is even more disjointed than the thoughts of Denver and Sethe. There is no punctuation and Morrison flouts typographical conventions, allowing the format of the text itself to endorse her choice of narrative style. This tactic, present in modern literature and poetry, and prefigured by earlier authors, for example Laurence Sterne (1713–68), further disorientate the reader. The replacement of full stops and other punctuation by spaces reflects the timelessness of Beloved's presence. Just as Sethe sees Beloved as hers, Beloved claims her mother as her own. They are the same person, and the syntactical confusion does much to convey this blurring of personal boundaries: 'she is my face smiling at me'. The section presents a muddled regurgitation of many of the previous episodes in which Beloved has featured. There are references to turtles, earrings, her appearance, and to an iron circle which reminds the reader of the choking incident and also of a slave collar. Morrison has explained in an interview with Marsha Darling (*Conversations with Toni Morrison*, edited by Danille Taylor Guthrie, 1994) that Beloved speaks the languages of both Death and the Middle Passage and that the language is the same for both experiences.

SECTION 5 PAGES 214–17

Chorus of the women's voices

A more coherent version of Beloved's thoughts is presented. An exchange between Sethe and Beloved is related in the form of a series of questions and answers. Sethe asks her daughter if she has forgiven her and promises to protect her. A similar exchange between Denver and Beloved takes place. Denver too offers to protect Beloved, and warns her against Sethe. The three female voices join together in a chorus. The voice that we associate with Beloved is increasingly resentful. She accuses Sethe of leaving her, of not smiling and of hurting her. They reiterate the fact that they all belong to each other.

The use of a chorus, a musical device, is a tribute to the importance of music for black heritage. Morrison is very aware of the musicality of black language and speech. This is present in her other novels, for example *Jazz*, in which the structural principle is music. The themes of milk and blood are those which interlace the novel.

SECTION 6 PAGES 218–29

Paul D remembers Sixo's death and the last scenes at Sweet Home

Paul D is sitting on the church steps, drinking whisky and abandoning himself to thoughts of his past, in particular their plan of escape from Sweet Home, which was later complicated by Halle's new working arrangements, the increasing demands of Mrs Garner, Sethe's pregnancy and the fact that Sixo was kept tied up at night. Once again he questions his manhood, and wonders whether it is merely a word conferred upon him by Mr Garner. He remembers the confusion that befell their attempted escape. He was separated from his brothers, and he and Sixo were caught by schoolteacher. The white men discussed the price that he would fetch on the slave market. Sixo retaliated and the white men tried to set fire to him. The wood was wet and Sixo laughed and sang. They shot him. His last triumphant shout was 'Seven-O'. The Thirty-Mile-Woman had escaped and was pregnant with his child. Paul D remembers how he was shackled and wearing a neck collar when Sethe came to see him to ask about Halle. She had already sent her children away. This is the scene that Paul D remembered in the first section. It preceded her violation and the beating she received in the barn.

Morrison returns to a more traditional narrative. Paul D's tobacco tin heart is overflowing and he is the 'play and prey' of his thoughts (p. 118). There are other examples of word play and **assonance** throughout the novel, for example 'leaving ... living' (p. 4). His fascination and envy of established black communities is discussed in Recurring Themes and Imagery, on Community and Family. Paul D reflects on the power of language and naming in relation to his manhood. He thinks of his 'value' in terms of work, but discovers his 'worth' in terms of 'price'.

The story of leaving Sweet Home is picked up. The word 'But' is repeated, as a prefix to the list of all the hitches to their plan (p. 223). When Halle hears the 'sign' for their departure he transforms it into a song, just as Paul D and the others on the chain gang used songs to communicate. Using Spirituals to name the dynamics of an escape has a long African-American history. Martin Luther King (in his 1967 Canadian Broadcasting Corporation Massey Lecture Series) described the spirituals as 'codes' and explained how the Spiritual, 'Follow the Drinking Gourd' contained the directions for escape. The gourd signified the constellation of the Plough and the North Star to which its handle pointed gave a celestial map that indicated the way of flight to the Canadian border.

Sixo's last laugh is finally put into context.

dry-goods church the church's premises had once been a shop
tackroom room for storing horses' harnesses
doggone (exclamation) damned
juba rhythmic African dancing and singing
buckboard open horse-drawn carriage

SECTION 7 PAGES 230–5

Stamp tells Paul D that he can stay with any black family and explains the origin of his name. Paul D tells Stamp about Beloved

Stamp Paid finds Paul D on the church steps, and apologises to him for the nights that he has spent there, offering him the use of any coloured person's house in the neighbourhood. He offers to rectify any damage he has caused. He tells Paul D how he got his name. Before choosing the name of Stamp Paid, he was called Joshua. The man for whom he worked took his wife, Vashti, for his own sexual purposes. Stamp thought about killing his owner and also his wife. In the end they escaped and he renamed himself. Stamp tries to explain Sethe's motives when she killed her daughter. Paul D tells him about Beloved, and asks him, overcome by the misery of their lives: 'How much is a nigger supposed to take?'

Stamp Paid challenges white power by renaming himself. This self-baptism is an assertion of self-worth and self-ownership and therefore a direct refutation of slavery. His name alludes to the subtext of commercial exchange that informs the novel, the pricing of Paul D and the other slaves, or Denver's fear that she owes something when she tells the story of her birth.

THREE

SECTION 1 PAGES 239–62

> **Denver realises that her mother is in danger. She plucks up the courage to leave 124. The community start leaving her food. Denver goes to the Bodwins and is hired. The women of the community decide to intervene to rescue Sethe from Beloved. Mr Bodwin arrives to pick up Denver and when Sethe sees him she attacks him with an ice-pick**

The situation in 124 Bluestone Road has degenerated. Sethe has stopped going to work, and is getting more and more emaciated, while Beloved swells in size. Denver is excluded from their games and struggles for power. Beloved blackmails Sethe, reminding her of what she did, and Sethe serves her daughter. Denver's allegiance changes: she moves from wanting to protect Beloved to fearing for her mother's safety. Sethe becomes ill and Denver realises that she is the one who will have to leave the house and do something to save the situation. She is frightened at the thought of this, but she hears the voice of Baby Suggs, and plucks up the courage to call on Lady Jones at the house in which she used to receive lessons. Denver asks for help, and from then on she begins to find gifts of food in the woods near her home. Scraps of paper are attached indicating the owner of the dishes or the donor of the present. She goes to thank her neighbours and in this way becomes reintegrated with the world outside the house. She hears people talk about the happy times they enjoyed at 124.

Meanwhile Sethe and Beloved have swapped roles, and Sethe is becoming as weak as a baby. Denver realises that Beloved is making Sethe pay for her actions, while Sethe is trying to compensate for what she did. Beloved is the only person whom she feels she has to convince.

Denver has become completely insignificant in this stalemate situation, and realises that she has to go out to look for work. She goes to see the Bodwins for help. In exchange for information about the reality of her home life, the woman who works there, Janey, agrees to help Denver to get work with the Bodwins. She suggests that Denver stay there at night. Janey tells all the other neighbours that Sethe's dead daughter has come back to haunt her, inflating Denver's reserved account. Ella hears this tale and determines to come to Sethe's rescue.

As Denver is sitting waiting for Mr Bodwin to come and pick her up for her first night at work, thirty women come to 124 Bluestone Road. They pray and sing.

As he drives the cart, Mr Bodwin, now seventy years old, thinks of the house in which he was born and recalls the time when he was an active abolitionist, working against the evils of slavery.

The women gathered about 124 Bluestone Road see Sethe and Beloved in the yard. Sethe is breaking ice into chunks. Beloved is naked, glistening and swollen like a pregnant woman. Sethe looks up and sees the approach of Mr Bodwin. She feels the hummingbirds in her hair, and sees a white man coming into her yard. Still holding the ice-pick she runs out of the yard, determined to protect her daughters.

Lady Jones's self-hatred, exquisitely developed in a paragraph or so, refers to the problems of having a white identity within the black spectrum. (Colourism, or prejudice by the black community against its own members – yet another challenge to the survival of black identity – is given a more prominent role in Toni Morrison's other novels, in particular, *Song of Solomon*, *Sula* and *Paradise*.)

The word 'baby', is what makes Denver a woman, just as the words pronounced by Nelson Lord caused her deafness and his words addressed to her as an adult 'opened her mind' (p. 252). Denver is susceptible to language, and her reintegration into the community is signposted by writing and scraps of paper.

The description of the waiting women outside 124 is followed by a section of Bodwin's thoughts. His vanity and self-satisfaction allow the narrative to lose tension momentarily, thereby increasing the impact of the final scene. The phrase describing the blue of the sky (p. 261) is exactly the same as that used by Baby Suggs when she smells disapproval (p. 138) prior to Sethe's desperate retreat into the woodshed. The play on words of the sound sounding, is followed by the references to the pods of chestnut trees which throws the reader back to Sethe's memories of the Clearing (pp. 94, 164). Sethe's impassioned and musical 'no' and the **metaphor** of the attacking hummingbirds provides an exact repetition of the passage in Section 18 where her behaviour in the woodshed is finally explained. There 'she flew' to destroy her own offspring, now 'she flies' to annihilate Bodwin, who represents the perpetrator of violence against black women, the 'man without skin' (p. 262) from Beloved's monologue (pp. 210–2).

She was wild game Beloved is unpredictable. She does not abide by societal or familial rules

rout Baby Suggs uses this word to imply the utter impossibility of any kind of struggle between black and white people, when the latter possess all the power and resources

chippy prostitute, sexually promiscuous woman

Settlement Fee the fee for being allowed to take up residence

junked shunned her socially. Other than nodding at Sethe at the carnival section, Ella had not spoken to Sethe in eighteen years

Cobbler an iced drink made from wine, sugar and fruit juice

harps Jews' harps – musical instruments played like a mouth organ

brake ... bell instruments used to restrain slaves

in the beginning was the sound a revision of the Scriptures, 'in the beginning was the Word'

the Society a reference to the American Anti-Slavery Society, formed in 1833 in Philadelphia

the Secessionists those states that decided to withdraw from the Union, that is, the rebel or Confederate States

SECTION 2 PAGES 263–73

Beloved is gone. Paul D meets Denver. He remembers his travels after Alfred and his first experience of the North. He goes to visit Sethe

Beloved has gone. Some people say that she just disappeared, while others claim that she exploded in front of their eyes. Paul D is convinced of her departure because the dog, Here Boy, has returned to the house. Mr Bodwin is trying to sell the house: it transpires that Sethe tried to stab Mr Bodwin with the ice-pick, and was prevented by Ella hitting her. Mr Bodwin saw Beloved, but the women deny her existence. Paul D and Stamp agree that he must also have seen that Sethe was trying to reach him, but, luckily, he chose not to acknowledge it.

The next day Paul D sees Denver. She is thinner and looks very much like Halle. Her answers to Paul D are civil and she seems to have grown up. Miss Bodwin had been teaching her and she is looking for an afternoon job to supplement her wages and support her mother. Paul D asks her if she thinks that Beloved was her sister, and she does not answer him directly. She tells him to be careful of the way in which he treats Sethe. Paul D remembers his attempted escapes and the various ways in which he was frustrated. He recalls the freedom he experienced in Trenton and the first money that he earned. He goes to 124 Bluestone Road to look for Sethe. She is lying in Baby Suggs's bed singing to herself. Paul D is angry to see her without strength, and realises that she has given up in the way that Baby Suggs did. He tells her that he is going to look after her, and starts by washing her. She looks at him and cries. Beloved, her 'best thing' has left her. He tells her that she herself is her best thing, and that they ought to stay together.

Paul D asks Sethe what she is planning and she declares that she has 'no plans at all' (p. 273). The absence of plans denotes the lack of a future. In the third section of One, Denver describes her vision of a floating dress and interprets it as the baby's plans (p. 37). Sethe, years later, remembers Denver's words and, with Paul D asleep beside her, thinks of the implications of the word (p. 39). Plan-making is regarded as a luxury, since the one plan that she did make went so disastrously wrong. This plan, was, of course, the escape from Sweet Home, which is described by Paul D in the same terms (pp. 223–4). The impossibility of making plans is linked with the power of memories of the past. Sethe has 'no room to imagine, let alone plan for, the next day' (p. 70). Thus Paul D's declaration that he and Sethe must create 'some kind of tomorrow' (p. 273) expresses the hope that having exorcised the past, embodied by the carnal manifestation of Beloved, they can gain access to the future and to the right to plan.

This penultimate section is replete with repetitions. Paul D's ability to make women cry is described with the same words as in the first section: 'because with him, in his presence, they could' (pp. 272, 17). The composite nature of the narrative fills the text with past references and phrases. For example, Paul D uses the phrase 'Devil's confusion', just as he replied on the occasion of their first meeting (pp. 271, 7) or the reference to bathing in sections, as performed by Baby Suggs (pp. 272, 93).

Oberlin Oberlin College was founded before the Civil War in 1833. It was the first college in the States to adopt coeducation, and in 1835 it admitted students 'without respect to color'. It was a noted centre for anti-slavery sentiments

Rebellers another word for the Confederate states

Confederate the name adopted by those states that seceded and formed an independent union at the end of 1860 and the beginning of 1861. The Civil War was their fight against the Federate Government of the North

Yankees Union soldiers during the Civil War

Union the Union was the name given to the Northern States

skiff a light rowing boat

SECTION 3 PAGES 274–5

> **An epilogue in the third person describes the way in which Beloved and the memory of her passed from the protagonists' lives. The novel finishes with her name.**

The novel is open-ended and the reader is denied a sense of resolution. The story of Beloved in not one to be 'passed on' although that is exactly what Morrison has done.

Disremembered a word coined by Morrison to imply 'forgotten'. The prefix 'dis' makes it seem like a deliberate activity: a conscious choice not to remember. This is quite different from the unconscious process with which we usually associate 'forgetting'

to pass on this has a double meaning: 'to retell' or 'to skip'

PART THREE

CRITICAL APPROACHES

CHARACTERISATION

SETHE

Sethe is a pivotal character in *Beloved*. The narrative voice of the novel is most often hers as she relives and 'rememories' the awfulness of her life as a slave.

She rarely saw her mother, and was brought up by a one-armed woman named Nan, while her mother worked in the fields (pp. 30, 60) as a slave. Her mother took her aside one day to show her a mark which was branded on her ribcage. Later Sethe finds her mother hanged, along with many other women, but she never discovers the reason why. Sethe is presumably a second-generation slave, since she can remember her mother speaking another language (p. 62) and being told of her repeated rapes during the voyage to America. Sethe's memories of her youth are vague, but at the age of thirteen she is sold to Sweet Home, a farm in Kentucky. She is bought to replace Baby Suggs, whose son she later marries and to whose home she escapes.

While Sweet Home is run by Mr Garner and his wife, Sethe lives in relative tranquillity. She works in the kitchen and makes ink for Mr Garner. All five of the male slaves would like her as a partner, but after a year she chooses Halle to be her husband. They make love in a cornfield to spare the feelings of the other slaves, but the waving of the corn on a windless day signals their activity to the watching men. She gets pregnant every year and has three children, two boys named Howard and Buglar, and a baby girl. She is nineteen and pregnant for the fourth time when Mr Garner dies.

His brother-in-law (schoolteacher) comes to take control of the farm. From this point onwards life becomes unbearable for the slaves. They decide to escape, but in the ensuing confusion Sethe is forced to send her three children on ahead to Baby Suggs's house. After being beaten mercilessly by the nephews, and having to endure the indignity of their sucking milk from her swollen breasts, she runs away on foot. She gives birth to her fourth child (Denver) with the help of a white girl named Amy, is helped to cross the Ohio river and reaches 124 Bluestone Road where her mother-in-law, Baby Suggs, is living. For twenty-eight days she enjoys freed life before schoolteacher arrives to take her and her children back to Sweet Home. Rather than allow this to happen, she takes her children into the woodshed and tries to kill them all, to preserve them from a life of hopeless slavery.

The intolerable nature of her life is no different from that of many other black characters in the novel. The difference lies in her dramatic response. Various characters try to dissuade her from loving too much (pp. 45, 92). Paul D describes her love as 'too thick', and recognises that to love in such a way is 'risky', given the precarious nature of slave existence (p. 45). Nevertheless, her daughter Denver and the spirit of her dead baby, Beloved, become the focus of her life: she will not allow Paul D to criticise them, she gives up her job and centres her world within the walls of 124 Bluestone Road. She succeeds in despatching her best thing – her small daughter – to safety by cutting her throat with a handsaw. She sees this act as one of protection and provision for her young but, paradoxically, it proves to be an act of destruction, lending gruesome **irony** to the phrase, 'mother love was a killer' (p. 132).

Sethe is impressively strong. Her determination manifests itself in her successful escape from Sweet Home. Pregnant and wounded she manages to make her way through the woods and across the Ohio river. Although haunted by her memories of the past, she withstands the humiliation of being sexually abused by two men. Halle witnesses this and loses his reason. He is last seen beside the butter churn, spreading butter on his face. She thinks for a moment that it would have been a release if she too could have joined him, but her three children on the way to Ohio needed her and 'no butter play would change that' (p. 71). Sethe's strength is embodied in her remarkable eyes and unflinching gaze. This is the quality that Denver accepts as intrinsic to her mother: Sethe does not look away from a variety of ghastly sights (p. 12). Paul D is similarly struck by her 'polished' eyes (p. 25). When she is on the verge of leaving Sweet Home, she kneels by Paul D and the fire, and he notices the complete absence of expression in her face. Schoolteacher thinks that she looks blind when he sees her in the woodshed (p. 151).

Until Beloved's physical manifestation, Sethe copes with the guilt of her own act and cohabits with her baby daughter's spirit. However, for all her strength, Sethe is beaten by Beloved. She is punished and allows herself to be swamped by her guilt. Mother and daughter become involved in a terrible deadlock of love. Nevertheless, the final exorcism of Beloved and the return of Paul D seem to imply the possibility of a future, and Denver is instrumental in reintroducing Sethe into the community from which she has been an exile. Her last words, 'Me? Me?' (p. 273) promise a new life for Sethe in which she, absolved of her guilt, can value herself as her own best thing.

B ELOVED

Morrison told PBS host Charlie Rose that one of the questions that prompted her novel was 'Who is the beloved?' Several literary critics have devoted their attention to asking, 'Who is Beloved?' Is the ghostly child a supernatural succubus, or vampire, or a real person who appears and chooses to accept the identity that Sethe is determined to foist upon her? The name Beloved is that on the baby's grave, but not that of Sethe's own daughter. It is a word used both at funerals and weddings, thus signifying both past and future. Beloved can also be seen as the embodiment of slavery itself.

If Beloved is Sethe's executed daughter come back to life, then she is willed into existence by the women of 124 Bluestone Road. Sethe announces ominously that if her daughter would only come back she would be able to explain her actions to her (p. 4). Denver craves companionship and treasures her sister's presence, both ghostly and actual. But Denver is to learn that she is of little importance to Beloved. After the departure of Paul D, Beloved and Sethe engage in a tug of love, guilt and retribution. Beloved lacks the ability to forgive her mother for her crime, echoing Sethe's own inability to forgive herself.

Although Beloved arrives at 124 Bluestone Road as an adult, we witness her living through the human life cycle. At first her needs are for oral gratification and her mother's gaze. She is unable to bear the weight of her own head and cannot walk or talk properly. At this point she is developmentally and emotionally an infant. She remains at the stage of primary identification, refusing to differentiate herself from her mother: 'her face is my own' (p. 210). During her stay she becomes a vindictive and unrelenting teenager, untouched by the usual rules that regulate a parent-child relationship. Beloved takes emotional advantage of Denver by befriending her, and physical advantage of Paul D by seducing him. She becomes Sethe's judge and begins to take her over. She wears her clothes, imitates her, and laughs 'her laugh' (p. 241). Denver begins to have difficulty in telling them apart, as Beloved dominates Sethe, swelling in size as her mother shrinks. A physical embodiment of the spiteful poltergeist, Beloved is a malignant presence, who would as soon strangle Sethe as soothe her.

Crucially absent from the text is any explanation by the author of why Beloved appears, where she goes after her disappearance or whether she really disappears. Ella is 'not so sure' that she will not return (p. 263). The novel presents the reaction of others to her presence; by the epilogue she is forgotten. Not one of the characters can remember anything that she said, and it is posited that perhaps she only said and thought what they themselves were thinking (p. 274). This allows a psychoanalytical reading of Beloved's presence: as the incarnation of Sethe's sense of guilt and her unforgiving memory, with which she has to come to terms before she can accept the future that Paul D offers. Beloved can also be seen as America's past of slavery, with her memories of the Middle Passage, haunting the reader in the same way as it haunted Toni Morrison herself before she embarked on the novel that took her six years to write. Although Beloved's presence is a negative one, it purges the guilt-ridden Sethe, who needs punishment in order to gain redemption. Denver recounts the way in which her mother seems to provoke Beloved's outrages (p. 252), with a masochistic desire for penance.

DENVER

Denver is a minor character, without a past, and excluded from the shared pain of the older **protagonists**. Her birth is something that happened to Sethe and, although Denver loves the story, when she tells it she switches from a third-person narrative to experiencing it as Sethe. Her narrative is overpowered by the past and her voice is drowned. So much of the novel depends on the life at Sweet Home, its dissolution and consequences, that Denver is set aside. She herself is aware of the bond that unites Paul D and her mother and resents it ferociously.

Denver is the character most sensitive to Beloved and her true identity. She drank her sister's blood along with Sethe's milk (p. 152), much to Baby Suggs's horror. As a child, as 'lonely and rebuked' as she claims that the ghost is (p. 13), she plays with Beloved, and her deafness is broken by the sound of the baby girl trying to crawl up the steps. She needs Beloved in the same way that Beloved needs Sethe, and we witness her desolation when Beloved disappears in the cold house (pp. 122–3). She feels that she has lost her self, and it is only when she takes responsibility for her own life at the instigation of Nelson Lord that she realises she has a self of her own 'to look out for and preserve' (p. 252).

In many ways, the advent of Beloved is a catalyst for a development in Denver's character and way of living. Nursing their sick guest makes her become patient, while her desire to capture Beloved's attention and divert her makes her become dutiful in the house, inventing chores to do together to pass the time. In the deadlock of love in which Beloved and Sethe finally become involved, Denver realises that she is of no importance. Originally prepared to protect Beloved from her saw-wielding mother, she now realises that she must save her mother from Beloved. She reacts, not with the sullen resentment she feels when Paul D arrives, but as an adult. She is forced to leave the yard and find work. When Paul D meets her in the penultimate section of the novel she is composed and mature. She is searching for a second job, and treats, and is treated by, Paul D as a fellow adult. Finally she is successful in breaking out of the narrowly defined, self-destructive circle of family relationships in 124 Bluestone Road.

PAUL D

In the penultimate section, Paul D tells Sethe that 'we got more yesterday than anybody' (p. 273). Together with Sethe, Paul D provides the details of oppression and suffering that are the context and justification for Sethe's dramatic gesture in the woodshed. The description of his past prompts some of the more historically **allusive** passages in this novel: his experience in the Civil war, travel to the North and time spent at the prison camp. Paul D's narrative voice gives us the chilling details of Sixo's death, the humiliation of 'neck jewellery' and of white domination, until we are forced to echo his desperate words on the church steps: 'How much is a nigger supposed to take?' (p. 235).

After the break-up of Sweet Home, he attempted to kill his new owner and was taken to a prison camp. He escaped, along with other members of the chain gang and they found themselves in a camp of Cherokee Indians. He was the last of the men to leave the Cherokee camp. He goes North, fights on both sides of the Civil War and spends eighteen months in Delaware with a weaver woman. He envies extended families, having been denied roots by the system of slavery. The same system undermines his sense of manhood so that he feels dispossessed. Although he loves the land and is moved by its texture, he is fully aware that he has no right to it (p. 221).

Despite his dreadful experiences, he is a generous and loving man, with an ability to provoke emotions in others. There is 'something blessed in his manner' (p. 17): within minutes of his entry into 124 Bluestone Road both Sethe and Denver cry, and Sethe weeps again in the penultimate section of the book (p. 272). At the carnival his good humour is infectious (p. 48). He has learned to focus his affection on inanimate objects: 'loving small and in secret' (p. 221) and he is disturbed by the intensity and power of Sethe's love. He leaves Sethe after Stamp Paid tells him about her murderous act, not because of what she did, but because of the way in which she justifies it. His dream of creating a family unit with her is ruined. He realises that Sethe is much stronger than he had imagined, and that she is not like Halle.

His relationship with Beloved is antagonistic. One of his first acts on arrival at the house is to drive the ghost out of it. He resents and questions the presence of the full-grown Beloved, 'a room-and-board witch' (p. 164) and interrogates her about her origins. She moves him out of Sethe's bed and seduces him in the cold house. He responds by telling Sethe that he would like to father her child. She gives him a feeling of rootedness. He tells Sethe that when he arrived at her porch he realised (p. 46) that he had been heading towards her and is convinced that they can make a life together. Before, it was sufficient to 'eat, walk and sleep anywhere' (p. 270), but he is moved by Sethe, and wants to live out his life with her (p. 221). The sealed tobacco tin that is a **metaphor** for his heart breaks open and his suppressed memories fly free. Their pasts are complementary: 'he wants to put his story next to hers' (p. 273) and the possibility of their having a future together necessitates coming to terms with their shared and traumatic past. Like Sethe, Paul D had limited himself to a fulfilment of immediate exigencies and nothing more. When he was roaming America, thinking 'only about the next meal and night's sleep ... he had no sense of failure, of things not working out. Anything that worked out at all, worked out' (p. 221). Similarly, Sethe believes that her present life with Denver is better precisely because it is not 'that other one' (p. 42). The two of them are forced to confront each other's past and it is this confrontation that gives the novel its force.

BABY SUGGS

Although Baby Suggs is dead, she is a prominent character. She is missed and alluded to by many of the **protagonists**. Paul D asks after her in the very first section, and Sethe, upon hearing that Halle is dead, longs for the comfort of her massaging fingers. Janey, the servant of the Bodwins, for all her scathing remarks about Sethe and her behaviour, has only 'sweet words' (p. 254) for Baby Suggs. For Denver, the death of her grandmother is one of several losses, and she remembers Baby Suggs telling her stories about her father and promising her that the baby ghost would not hurt her (pp. 207–9). Stamp Paid was originally angry with Baby Suggs's resignation from the world. Later in the novel he comes to understand her final defeatist stance (p. 177):

> sixty years of losing children to the people who chewed up her life ... five years of freedom given to her by her last child, who bought her future with his ... to lose him too; to acquire a daughter ... see that daughter slay the children (or try to); to belong to a community of ... free Negroes ... and then have that community step back and hold itself at a distance – well, it could wear out even a Baby Suggs, holy.

Baby Suggs had eight children by six different fathers. Scattered through the narrative are **allusions** to the pain of never seeing one's children grow. She never saw any of her four daughters in adulthood (p. 139). The people she has known have all 'run off ... been hanged, got rented out, loaned out, bought up, brought back, stored up, mortgaged, won, stolen or seized' (p. 23). After Halle has bought her her freedom she tries to reunite her family, but her efforts are thwarted. She focuses all her remaining affection upon Halle and his new family. Baby Suggs's life is a practical example of the brutality of the slave system: the way men and women were moved around like draughts on a board. This is exemplified by the way that her employers misname her for the duration of her working life. She is one of the many women in the narrative who have suffered some degree of sexual abuse. She recounts briefly the way in which she was blackmailed and betrayed by a 'straw boss' who coerced her into 'coupling' with him. He then sold the son that he had fathered (p. 23). Similarly the overseer of the over-full ship, in which her two daughters Nancy and Famous perished, brings her the news of their deaths in the hopes of 'having his way with her' (p. 144) rather than through any altruism.

Her son pays for her freedom. As a slave she has no self, denied of 'the map to discover what she was like' (p. 140). She has been dispossessed of her sense of identity, and, only upon being freed does she regain it. In the carriage, she feels her heart beating for the first time. Liberated from oppression, she becomes a formidable and strong woman. While she lives at 124 Bluestone Road it is a focal point for the community: 'a cheerful, buzzing house where Baby Suggs, holy, loved, cautioned, fed, chastised and soothed' (pp. 86–7). When Denver begins to meet her neighbours she is regaled with tales of 124 Bluestone Road (p. 249) as it used to be. In Part One, Section 9, Sethe describes the services that Baby Suggs held in the Clearing, which earned her the right to be called 'holy'. Her 'great heart' (p. 87) beats in the presence of men, women and children, and she speaks a subversive message of self-love and worthiness. She urges her hearers to love themselves, in contrast to their evaluation by white people: 'And O my people they do not love your hands. They only use, tie, bind, chop off and leave empty' (p. 88). She gave Denver the same message, authorising her right to 'pleasurable feelings' (p. 209) and commanding her to love and respect her body. She was a central figure in the community, but, after Sethe's actions she gave up her role of 'unchurched preacher' and retreated to her bed in order to contemplate colour – to indulge in a little sensuousness – regressing to a child-like state. The fact that the system of slavery and the Fugitive Bill permitted schoolteacher to enter her yard to fetch Sethe – thus precipitating the terrible chain of events – results in Baby Suggs losing faith in the God she had believed in. Denver paraphrases what her grandmother felt: 'she had done everything right and they came in her yard anyway' (p. 209). The Civil War and the disappearance of her grandsons hardly affect her; instead there is her quiet devotion to colour, which she admires because it does not 'hurt' anything.

For all her strength and wisdom, she is destroyed by Sethe's actions, a fact that Sethe herself acknowledges (p. 183). The last years of her life and her last words show her awareness of the terrible power that white people had over black. The destruction of a woman renowned and loved for her heart, the one thing left intact (p. 87) after a life of slavery, is as tragic as Sethe's reaction to that institution. Baby Suggs cannot even be buried in the Clearing due to a rule invented by whites (p. 171) and her funeral is a scene of divisive spite. Before dying she informs Sethe and Denver that: 'there is no bad luck in the world but whitefolks' (p. 89). She holds them responsible for breaking her heart, for stealing all that she owned or for which she dreamed.

MINOR CHARACTERS

STAMP PAID

Stamp Paid has a key role in the novel's events. He is the man who meets Sethe and ferries her across the Ohio. He brought the blackberries that started the feast that overstepped the boundaries of propriety. Baby Suggs's extravagant generosity caused bad feeling that prevented the community from warning the inhabitants of 124 about schoolteacher's approach. Once more, he is there the next morning, chopping wood as the white men arrive to remove Sethe and the children. He saw Denver shortly after she was born and saved her from being killed by Sethe: he is fond of her. He shows Paul D the newspaper clipping about Sethe, thus precipitating Paul D's departure. It is the thought of Denver, combined with the memory of Baby Suggs that prompts him to try to remedy the damage he has caused through telling Paul D about Sethe.

The tale of Stamp's life, which he recounts to Paul D, demonstrates yet another way in which white people sullied the lives of black people. After his wife, Vashti, was taken from him to please his master's son, Stamp renames himself with his present name. Before, he was called Joshua. His choice of a new name, 'Stamp Paid', signifies that he considers himself responsible for his own salvation, that he is debt-free and has no remaining obligations. He devotes the rest of his life to helping others. His payment is always being a welcome visitor, never having to knock on a door. His sense of community is fully developed, as is evidenced by his anger with Ella when he discovers that Paul D has been dossing in the church cellar.

Stamp was a friend of Baby Suggs, and saw her as a woman with the strength of a mountain (p. 181). He realises that he was wrong to upbraid her, and comes to understand her resignation, and why ultimately she renounced her religious duties.

ELLA

Like Stamp Paid, Ella helps fugitives to safety. She meets Sethe at the other side of the Ohio river. Although she had been friends with Baby Suggs, after Sethe's behaviour she does not speak to her, and in eighteen years has only nodded to her at the carnival. She has no patience with Sethe's pride. 'I ain't got no friends take a handsaw to their own children' (p. 187). Despite her strong stance, it is Ella who goes to Sethe's rescue. She goes to exorcise Beloved and, when Sethe tries to kill Mr Bodwin, she knocks her out. She is prompted to help Sethe by a fear of 'past errors taking hold of the present' (p. 256). For the same reasons that she disapproves of Sethe's behaviour, she cannot condone Beloved's return and her unrelenting destruction of her mother. Stamp Paid reproaches her for not offering Paul D a bed after he left Sethe's house (p. 186). We learn that she was shared by a white father and his son (p. 256), whom she refers to as 'the lowest yet'. Ella sees life as a 'test and a trial' (p. 256) and has been beaten 'every way but down' (p. 258).

LADY JONES

Lady Jones runs the school that Denver once attended. Denver returns to Lady Jones's house when she realises that she needs to help Sethe. She is of mixed race, and has grey eyes and 'yellow woolly hair' (p. 247). Her light skin means that she was allowed the benefit of education and she teaches the children of the area for a nickel a month. This is done in the spirit of retaliation: Lady Jones despises herself for not being entirely black, and assumes that this feeling is shared by the rest of the community. She does not share the awe for Baby Suggs that the other characters express, referring to her in her thoughts as 'the ignorant grandmother'. She is one of the women who scorns the supernatural story of Beloved's return to 124 Bluestone Road.

MR AND MRS GARNER

Mr Garner is the proprietor of Sweet Home and of six slaves: Sethe, Halle, Paul D, Paul F, Paul A and Sixo. He prides himself on his liberal attitude (pp. 10–11): he believes *his* slaves are men, in contradistinction to his neighbours' – 'Y'all got boys' (p. 11). Baby Suggs, Sethe's predecessor, recognises the 'special kind of slavery' (p. 140) where Garner treats them as if they were employees. She remembers the smallness of Sweet Home and the fact that 'nobody knocked her down' (p. 139). She lists the incredible amount of tasks that she completes alongside Mrs Garner – before dismissing it with the phrase: 'nothing to it' (p. 140). Her work at Sweet Home is comparatively easy. Sethe works beside Mrs Garner in the kitchen and in the vegetable garden, and the two women, slave and owner, have a relationship of cooperation. Mrs Garner recognises Sethe's desire for some semblance of ceremony when she chooses Halle to be her partner, and gives Sethe a pair of crystal earrings as a present (p. 58). When Sethe is pregnant, a midwife is present. Mrs Garner gives Sethe a piece of cloth to make a dress for her baby (p. 163) and, when she is ill, Sethe nurses Mrs Garner as if she were her mother (pp. 193–5). When Sethe tells Mrs Garner about the beating she receives at the hands of schoolteacher's nephews (pp. 202, 228) Mrs Garner cannot stop crying.

While the female slaves are not forced to work in the fields and enjoy this relaxed relationship with their mistress, the men were allowed, encouraged to 'correct Garner, even defy him. To invent ways of doing things; to see what was needed and attack it without permission. To buy a mother, choose a horse or a wife, handle guns, even learn reading if they wanted to' (p. 125).

Mr Garner allowed Halle to buy his mother's freedom. He accompanies Baby Suggs to Cincinnati and introduces her to the Bodwins. Nevertheless he never questions the name on her bill-of-sale and calls her Jenny for the duration of her working life. He fully believes that he is responsible for the virility of his male salves, since he is: 'Tough enough and smart enough to make and call his own niggers men.' This reported speech is laden with the rooted attitudes that allowed slavery to exist. Garner, despite the respect with which he treats his slaves, regards them as possessions, 'his own niggers', whom he can shape with judicious treatment. While the slaves on Sweet Home appreciate Garner for his generosity, they realise the contradictions inherent in his attitude towards them. The **irony** is brought out by Halle, who points out the advantages for Garner in letting him buy Baby Suggs's freedom (pp. 195–6). As the Bodwins make clear, Garner's liberality is nevertheless a 'kind' of slavery (p. 145).

Mr Garner dies unexpectedly of a stroke and the whole structure of Sweet Home and the slaves' lives falls apart. As Paul D bitterly remembers: 'everything rested on Garner being alive ..., Now ain't that slavery, or what is it?' (p. 220). As soon as Mrs Garner is widowed she sells off one of Paul D's brothers; as a white woman, she must not be left alone with her slaves (p. 36). Her husband's brother-in-law, 'schoolteacher', arrives, 'to put things in order' (p. 9).

SCHOOLTEACHER
Schoolteacher is spelt throughout with a small 's'. This has an **ironic** significance: although he has a certain standing in white society and wields power over his slaves, this does not prevent them seeing him as a worthless person. Schoolteacher scorns Mr Garner's lax methods (p. 227). Schoolteacher devises a series of 'corrections' to reeducate the slaves, and records everything in his notebook (p. 221). He asks the slaves questions, and Sethe overhears him instructing his nephews to divide her animal and human characteristics (p. 193). Sethe realises that he is researching a 'book about us' (p. 37) and writing it with the ink that she makes. Schoolteacher represents the American intellectuals who, throughout the nineteenth century, found ways of justifying slavery with 'scientific' ratiocinations. He regards his slaves as little more than animals, with a biological ability to produce infinite labour for his farm. After Sethe's escape to Cincinnati and the dissolution of Sweet Home, schoolteacher appears at 124 Bluestone Road to repossess her (p. 148). The sight of him precipitates Sethe's drastic act in the woodshed, just as his attitude convinced her of the necessity of leaving Sweet Home: 'No notebook for my babies, and no measuring string neither' (p. 198). Schoolteacher's dehumanising and self-righteous behaviour epitomises one aspect of the evil of slavery.

THE BODWINS

Brother and sister, these are two Scots who have no sympathy with slavery. They are friends of Mr Garner, and once Baby Suggs's freedom has been bought, he takes her to see them in Cincinnati. They offer her the use of 124 Bluestone Road, and suggest that she mend shoes and take in washing for a living. When Sethe is imprisoned, it is only because of their exertions that she is not hanged. Denver is fully aware of their history of having helped her family when she goes to their house in the hope of finding work. There she sees a black boy ornament with its mouth crammed with pennies. The description of this ornament (p. 255) serves to underline that the Bodwins, for all their liberal attitudes, are nevertheless infected with racist modes of viewing black people. They agree to take Denver on as a night-help and Edward Bodwin drives to 124 to pick her up. He was born there and we hear his nostalgia for his childhood (p. 260) and his reflections on his adult life as an active abolitionist. It is a cruel **irony** that he should be the one whom Sethe attacks in her warped attempt to protect her daughters.

HALLE

Halle is the much-loved son of Baby Suggs. He took note of her pain and paid for her freedom with his own labour. He could read and count and was therefore able to calculate the worth of his work. He witnessed Sethe's rape when he was hiding in the barn, and was last seen by Paul D, rubbing butter over his face in the dairy. Baby Suggs claims that she felt him die on the day of Denver's birth (p. 8). Denver craves the father she has never known, listening avidly to her grandmother's anecdotes about him (p. 208) and envisaging a fantasy scenario in which he comes back to live with her and Beloved. The absence of information as to Halle's fate is a significant gap in the texture of Toni Morrison's narrative: 'Nobody knows what happened' (p. 224). This testifies to her commitment to illustrating a version of history that is very different from the cut-and-dried facts of history books – one that shows the messiness of real life.

SIXO

Sixo figures prominently in Paul D's memories of Sweet Home. He was the only one of the Sweet Home men who did not desire Sethe. Instead he planned to marry a woman who lived thirty miles away and Paul D relates his meetings with her (pp. 24, 222). Sixo represents the manhood that Paul D feels he is lacking, and it is significant that he imagines Sixo as his judge when he leaves Sethe (p. 267). Sixo is close to his tribal roots: he stops speaking English because he sees it as a language without a future and dances at night to keep his bloodlines open (p. 25). When he sings it is another language, but with 'hatred so loose it was juba' (p. 227). In the thwarted escape from Sweet Home, Sixo resists capture and is tied to a tree. Schoolteacher and the other men are unable to set him on fire, and have to shoot him to stop him singing (pp. 225–6). This act of violence is ostensibly recounted by Paul D. Its horror is not diminished by the use of narrative tricks but is told in a stark and chilling present tense.

AMY DENVER

Amy is an eighteen-year-old white girl who helps with Denver's birth and Sethe's survival. Significantly her name means friend or beloved. Her 'looking for velvet' is a search for sensuousness, softness in the North. She is the probable offspring of an indentured servant and her master. She is yet to have children, while Sethe, a year older, is pregnant with her fourth child. Although she is 'the raggediest looking trash you ever saw' (pp. 31–2) she travels at liberty while Sethe fears recapture and further violations.

Amy renames the marks on Sethe's back as a tree, transforming her scars from their association of death and pain to a thing of growth and beauty. Her chatter silences the baby and she wraps Sethe's feet. Together they form a temporary family unit of sorts in the absence of society's values, represented by the reference to 'no patroller' and 'no preacher' (p. 85). Amy leaves her mark in Denver's name. She is a primary instance of Toni Morrison's reluctance to vilify white people or valorise blacks, although by the end of the novel Sethe and Baby Suggs have no patience for any white people at all.

STRUCTURE

The novel is split into three parts of unequal length; with the first part subdivided into eighteen sections, the second into seven, and the third and an epilogue. All main parts open with a similar phrase, which draws attention to a progression in the state of events portrayed.

In the beginning, Sethe's home is rocked by Beloved's activities, limited at this point to poltergeist manifestations: '124 was spiteful' (p. 3). In One we witness the arrival and departure of Paul D, Beloved's appearance in flesh and blood and the awful events in the woodshed, related through the perceptions of a variety of protagonists. Although the narrative proceeds over the course of a year, the body of the text relates the events of the past. Two starts with the phrase: '124 was loud' (p. 169). The house is roaring with the voices of the oppressed, the 'people of the broken necks, of fire-cooked blood, and black girls who had lost their ribbons' (p. 181). This part contains **interior monologues** by Beloved, Sethe and Denver, and the latter two's acceptance of Beloved's identity as daughter and sister. It ends with Paul D's impassioned questioning of Stamp Paid as to how much suffering he, as a black man, is expected to withstand.

In Three, '124 was quiet' (pp. 239, 242). This part chronicles Denver's release into the world outside 124 Bluestone Road, while her mother and sister continue their battle of love and guilt. The lack of food and exhaustion subdues Beloved, and the house is quiet. Beloved disappears and Sethe takes to her bed. It closes with the possibility of a future life as Paul D returns to the house and pledges his commitment to a 'tomorrow' with Sethe.

The shortness of the sentence, containing just noun, verb and adjective, is significant. It imposes an order on the meandering narrative, the mixture of tenses, periods of time and first-person voices. The three key phrases underline the progression of events, and emphasise the location and development of these events in the immediate present of the novel as the house evolves through various stages, acting as a **symbol** for a similar evolution in the lives of its inhabitants.

TREATMENT OF TIME

The time-scale of *Beloved* is anything but linear. The narrative progresses in leaps and bounds, and stories are begun and left off, to be resumed again over the course of chapters. An example of this is the story of Denver's birth. It is begun by Denver in One, Section 3, resumed by

Denver in Section 8, but experienced through the persona of Sethe. The breaking of Sethe's waters has, however, already been alluded to earlier (p. 51), and Amy's description of the tree on her back is present in One, Section 1 (p. 16). Halfway through One, Section 9, the story continues, cataloguing Sethe's arrival at 124 Bluestone Road, and Baby Suggs's patient setting to rights of the damage done by the journey and the white boys. The same technique is used with the details of Sweet Home, Sethe and Halle's marriage, Stamp Paid's life or Paul D's experiences. The escape from Sweet Home is slowly pieced together.

LANGUAGE

In 1993 Toni Morrison was awarded the Nobel Prize for Literature. In her address she relates a story of an elderly blind woman, famed for her wisdom, which some children attempt to challenge, by presenting her with a bird. They ask her whether it is alive or dead. She answers by telling them that it is in their hands. Toni Morrison goes on to interpret this story as an **analogy** of a writer and the language she uses. What she says illustrates how fully she appreciates the power inherent in language both as a medium and an instrument. She acknowledges its complex properties and its capacity as a tool for and agent of oppression, but concludes by suggesting that the human capacity to 'do language' and to make meaning may be 'the measure of our lives'. Similarly in the preface to her critical work, *Playing in the Dark: Whiteness and the Literary Imagination* she comments on her awareness that 'language can powerfully evoke and enforce hidden signs of racial superiority, cultural hegemony, and dismissive "othering" of people and language'.

Beloved is testimony to Toni Morrison's manipulation of language. For example, when Paul D looks at Sethe, 'the word "bad" took on another meaning' (p. 7). Words can have different meanings, signs can have different '**signifieds**' (to use Saussure's phraseology). Sethe uses the word 'nurse' to describe the way she was forced to suckle two grown men, juxtaposing the idea of protection and love with the horror of the situation. A similar inappropriacy is found in the incongruous name, Sweet Home, which was neither 'sweet' nor 'home' for the slaves who lived there.

The protagonists' bodies convey a language of their own. Sethe, her mother and Beloved all bear scars that 'write' their slavery. The novel explores the way in which black women's bodies, as the site for reproduction, reveal stories of the past that were ignored in male slave-narratives. Paul D prevents Sethe from 'reading' the signs that mark Beloved as her daughter: the scar under her chin and the thin scratches on her forehead.

While Denver makes her link to the black community through writing (she goes to Lady Jones's house, where she first learned to read, and uses this skill to decipher the notes that are left with the food that her neighbours give her), non-written modes of communication bolster the narrative: the songs that Paul D sings as he mends the furniture, or works in the chain-gang, Amy's mother's song, or the song that Sethe has made up to sing to her children, and which Beloved is found singing. Above all, Toni Morrison mines the rich tradition of story-telling, that was so much a feature of black culture long before print existed and still is.

The substance of the novel, mediated largely via thoughts and spoken words, rarely takes the form of structured sentences. Instead, the narrative is peppered with rhetorical questions, semi-repetitions and half-sentences: it also jumps without warning from present to past and far past, all of which add verisimilitude and vitality.

As in music, where pauses and silence have an essential role, so here silence speaks volumes: 'Ella ... listened for the holes – the things fugitives did not say; the questions they did not ask. Listened too for the unnamed, unmentioned people left behind' (p. 92).

All Morrison's techniques draw attention to language's living properties, but there also exists a negative and deadening aspect of its power. Words are the cause of Denver's deafness: in order not to hear the answer that she dreads, she closes herself off from all sound. The illegible 'black scratches' (p. 155) of the newspaper that Stamp shows Paul D contain words that are powerless to explain Sethe's act (p. 161). Sixo stops speaking English because he sees no future in it (p. 25), illustrating the danger for the first Afro-Americans, condemned to creating their identity via a language that was not their own. Since slaves on their arrival in America came from a variety of ethnic groups and spoke different African languages they were forced to adopt English to communicate. In her speech when she received the Nobel Prize, Toni Morrison dwells on the susceptibility of language to death and erasure. Dead language is a danger that a writer must identify, and use techniques to avoid. *Beloved* is replete with such techniques.

STYLE

Toni Morrison uses the present tense throughout *Beloved*, although the narrative spans a period of some fifty years, stretching back to Baby Suggs's youth and Sethe's earliest memories of her mother. The prevalence and priority given to memories and remembering obscure the boundaries of time, so often used to structure literary works. Morrison flouts the confines of physical presence and consciousness by which novelists are usually restricted. While in her earlier novels she made use of premonitions, visions and coincidences, in *Beloved*, she unambiguously endorses the supernatural. One of the characters is a ghost. The novel, like the miserable house at 124 Bluestone Road, pulsates with unnatural energy.

Moreover, the readers are denied vital knowledge: we neither learn why Beloved has appeared, nor where she has gone. The shifting voice of the narrator, which flits in and out of different characters' thoughts, conveys a similar process of defamiliarisation for the reader. We hear the cogitations of Edward Bodwin (pp. 259–61), the thought processes of schoolteacher (pp. 149–51), and Stamp Paid's voice, as well as that of the central protagonists.

In Two there are four sections that represent the **interior monologues** of Sethe, Denver and Beloved. Those that belong to Beloved are most interesting when we come to consider the novel's style. The first of these is completely unpunctuated. Its language and content are highly repetitive and circular. It represents a time and place beyond the constructs of sentences and sense: the place from which Beloved came and where she existed as a spirit. It is possible to read this in terms of theories, appropriated by feminist critics, that children, before they succumb to the patriarchal dictates of formalised language, perceive the world through a female language that has an entirely different set of rules, shunning a linear time-scale, 'all of it is now' (p. 210) in favour of patterning. (For those interested, this can be traced via Freud, Lacan and Kristeva.) This supports our sense of Beloved being a baby. The technique is **stream of consciousness**. Here the style is accentuated, even on a typographical level, and disregards the common rules of writing. This style is not confined to Beloved's thoughts alone, but is used, to some extent, throughout. This means that there is no fixed point of reference for the reader, as memories meld and flow. Sethe's violent act in the woodshed is related from several different viewpoints: Baby Suggs, Stamp, schoolteacher and Sethe herself. We are given no indication as to whether we should approve or otherwise. We are forced to relive the same scene many times, and the facts of the baby's death are present from the very first pages.

These techniques and others mean that *Beloved* is open-ended. Morrison aspires to this quality and identifies incompletion as a feature of black music:

> Jazz always keeps you on the edge. There is no final chord ... Spirituals agitate you ... There is something underneath them that is incomplete ... I want my books to be like that ... I want that feeling of something held in reserve and the sense that there is more ... (N. McKay, 'An Interview with Toni Morrison')

Music is a rich source of **metaphor** for Morrison and is referred to in the preface of *Playing in the Dark*, as well as being used as a structural and thematic principle in her novel, *Jazz*. She aims to unsettle her readers by drawing their attention to the gaps in her narrative. Morrison states explicitly: 'I must use my craft to make the reader see the colours and hear the sounds' (see C. Tate, 'A Conversation with Toni Morrison'). Sound is central to her style of prose poetry, for example, the phrase: 'Sifting daylight dissolves the memory, turns it into dust motes floating in light' (p. 264) with its **assonance** of sibilant 's' sounds, and the hinted rhyme of 'motes ... float(ing)'.

Toni Morrison plays with repetition, a musical device, repeating memories and images, and, on a more local level, uses repetition as a device to recreate the thought processes of her characters. As in One, Section 1, where Denver reiterates Paul D's words: 'only those who knew him well ("knew him well")' and her own weariness 'wear her out. Wear her out' (p. 13). The same phrase is later repeated in the past tense (p. 29). In One, Section 2, sexual tension is built up by a highly eroticised account of the preparation of corn. The voyeurism in which Paul D and the other men engage while watching the corn move as Halle and Sethe have sex is reflected by a lingering and repetitive description of the way in which they prepare the damaged corn to eat that evening (p. 27). Sethe and Paul D's memories blend and fuse together. The phrase 'How loose the silk' is repeated four times with only one variation. The choral effect slows down the narrative, and recreates a sense of satiety. Repetition of a phrase is similarly used to create a sense of calm, as it imitates the rising and falling of Paul D's chest as he sleeps (p. 132), or to imbue a sense of panic when Paul D tells Stamp that the picture of Sethe is not her, since her mouth is drawn incorrectly. The phrase: 'That ain't her mouth' is repeated seven times (pp. 154–9) and does much to embody Paul D's stubborn refusal to accept Stamp's tale. When Sethe and the two girls go skating the phrase 'Nobody saw them falling' is repeated many times (p. 174) and effectively establishes the unity of the three women. This is one point in which the reader is made aware of their position as audience and outsider.

NARRATIVE TECHNIQUES

Toni Morrison's choice of narrative technique is very condensed. The **metaphors** are self-reflexive, referring to a context and experiences already established by the novel. When describing the pleasure Denver derives from being scrutinised by Beloved, the metaphor is consonant with Denver's own experience, and makes no reference to the outside world. Her skin grows soft and bright like 'the lisle dress that had her arms round her mother's waist' (p. 118). The reader recognises this reference to the vision that appeared to Denver (p. 29), and a series of links are forged within the novel's imagery. Similarly, characters refer to events that are explained much later to the reader. Paul D in Section 1, talking to Sethe about Halle, resolves that she need never know about her husband's dereliction by the butter churn (p. 8). The reference to the appalling scene of Halle by the churn makes no sense to the reader, but is later unpacked and given resonance (p. 69). Similarly the reference to Sixo's last laugh (p. 41) is later padded out (p. 229). This technique creates an intensity that cannot but be felt by the reader.

The Dehumanisation of Slaves

Beloved chronicles a period of radical change and redefinition for emancipated black people. As slaves they had been dependent on whites for their entire existence; they now found themselves without the material or emotional means to cope with freedom. Paul D describes with horror the black women, men and children that he saw before, during and after the Civil War (p. 66). He himself stole from pigs and 'fought owls' for food, whilst being hunted like a beast. He recalls a 'witless colored woman' who was under the delusion that ducks were her children. This confusion of boundaries is also present at Sweet Home, where, in the absence of women, the men were 'fucking cows' and had 'taken to calves' (pp. 10–11). It is perhaps this alignment of cows with women that makes Paul D's reproach to Sethe so powerful: she has two legs, not four, he says when she tells him of her attempted killing of her children.

Throughout, Toni Morrison makes telling use of vocabulary to highlight the boundaries and differences between animal and human. Sethe feels the indignity of being treated as a goat by schoolteacher's nephews, her swollen breasts milked by two grown men. Schoolteacher describes his slaves as if they were animals, albeit animals in his care. He regards Sethe as a creature that God has given him the responsibility of maintaining (p. 149). These common attitudes legitimised the dehumanising way in which white owners treated their slaves. That schoolteacher is convinced that black people are scarcely distinguishable from beasts is evinced by his research measurements and the conversation that Sethe overhears in which he requests his nephews to align her animal and human characteristics (p. 193). When schoolteacher witnesses what Sethe has done to her children in the woodshed, by attributing her behaviour to the excessive beating she received at the hands of his nephews, he makes an **analogy** with what would have happened had his nephews similarly beaten a horse or dog (p. 149).

The language of domestic animals, particularly horses, is often used by white people when describing their slaves. The planned escape from Sweet Home is described as a 'stampede' (p. 226); Sethe's youngest baby is referred to by the neutral noun 'foal' (p. 227), while Amy asks Sethe if she is just going to 'foal' (p. 33). Amy's casual acceptance of racial constructions and difference emphasises the racial hierarchy that persists even between two 'throw-away' people (pp. 84–5) such as herself and Sethe. Despite their moment of unity by the riverside, Amy's whiteness divides her from Sethe.

The dehumanisation of black slaves was embodied in the white attitude to their having children, the inevitable fruits of sex. Men and women were used to 'stud', and regarded as nothing more than a species of farm animal. Sethe is regarded as a valuable possession since she is 'property that reproduced itself without cost' (p. 228). As a woman she is capable of 'breeding' (pp. 149, 227) and furnishing the farm with new free labour. The more brutal aspects of slavery are hidden from the slaves while Mr Garner lives. Sethe is allowed the delusion of a wedding and honeymoon. Nevertheless, the importance of her capacity to produce is implicit in Mrs Garner's question when she learns that Sethe is getting married: 'Are you already expecting?' (p. 26). This attitude meant that black people were frequently prevented from enjoying sex or from loving their children, as Baby Suggs tells Denver: 'Slaves not supposed to have pleasurable feelings ... but they have to have as many children as they can to please whoever owned them' (p. 209).

The attitudes that permitted the studding of humans are consonant with those that allowed the destruction of family bonds and the selling of other human beings. Toni Morrison emphasises the utter depravity of slavery by underlining the concepts of humanity and bestiality.

NAMING

Choosing a name is an assertion of self-love and freedom, while the imposition of a name often implies a relationship of dominance and power. These themes have obvious links with the core issues of slavery and oppression.

White people have the power to define the slaves who work for them. Sixo attempts to use schoolteacher's own rationalisation to justify his theft of a young pig and is beaten to remind him that 'definitions belonged to the definers – not the defined' (p. 190). Paul D wonders whether he is a man or whether his manhood is something that Mr Garner has conferred on him. We learn that Garner prided himself on having men and not boys on his farm (pp. 10–11): 'Bought em thataway, raised em thataway', and regards himself as someone who is: 'tough enough and smart enough to make and call his own niggers men'. Here, in 'make and call', the processes of creation and naming are paralleled. A name announces an identity. When Paul D, wearing the bit, with his half-brothers gone and his plans for escape awry, sees a rooster strutting at liberty, he is struck by their relative positions. The rooster, ironically enough, is called 'Mister', an appellation that Paul D, as a slave, is unlikely to hear. Moreover, 'even if you cooked him, you'd still be cooking a rooster named Mister' (p. 72). Thanks to the actions of schoolteacher, Paul D feels that he has lost his own identity and he is even unsure of his manhood. The fact that schoolteacher denies his slaves the use of guns represents a symbolic emasculation: the guns can be read as phallic **symbols**. Schoolteacher and Garner share the same basic attitude; that the men who work for them are possessions, unformed substances that, with the right treatment, can be 'made' into men, or well-behaved beasts. Being a man and subsequent manliness is not inherent, but conferred. This linguistic relationship between giver and received, the namer and the named, reflects the power-relationship between the white owner and his black slaves. It is illustrated by the unimaginative and dehumanising names that Mr Garner gives the three half-brothers: Paul A, Paul D and Paul F. They are distinguished by a letter and no more. After he has left Sethe and is sitting on the church steps, Paul D contemplates this issue (p. 220):

> Garner called and announced them men – but only on Sweet Home, and by his leave. Was he naming what he saw, or creating what he did not? ... Did a whiteman saying it make it so?

He wonders what would have happened if Garner had taken the word away. Would he cease to be a man? The shifting nature of words and language and Paul D's insecurity have already been established in the first part of the book. Paul D lies next to Sethe and looks at her scarred back. He remembers his fondness for a tree he called 'Brother'. Here Paul D is exercising his own power of possession. By giving a tree a name he is making it his, in the same way that Sethe tried to personalise Mrs Garner's kitchen by decorating it with sprigs of herbs. He also recalls Sixo and his sixty-mile trip to see his woman. Paul D reflects: 'Now there was a man, and that was a "tree". Himself lying in the bed and the tree next to him, didn't compare' (p. 22). Words can have many levels of meaning and points of reference. The 'tree' on Sethe's back is not a tree although it is called so. Is Paul D not a man, although he has that name? Similarly Baby Suggs emphasises the importance of naming in relationships: 'A man ain't nothing but a man ... But a son? Well, now that's somebody' (p. 23).

The Garners call Baby Suggs by the name of her bill-of-sale, Jenny Whitlow, the surname being that of her former owner, in the same way a child takes its father's surname. This draws attention to the distorted paternal ethic that characterised slavery. Inhuman treatment was justified in the minds of white people because they saw their slaves as children or animals who needed guidance and could be trained and subdued.

Names can also be chosen. Stamp Paid rejects the name of Joshua, after having given up his wife to his master's son, and rechristens himself as an assertion of power. From then on he feels no obligation to anybody and devotes his life to helping others. Sethe's mother gives her the name of the only man she ever accepted, the only man she ever put her arms around. By doing so she commemorates her right to choose children and husband, in the same way that she exercises that right by throwing away the nameless children of the crew-members who violated her. Baby Suggs opts for the surname of the one man she regards as a husband, although six have fathered her children. She keeps the pet-name that he called her for a first name. Sethe calls her daughter after the strong-armed white girl who helped her. In naming her baby after Amy, Sethe acknowledges the white girl as kin responsible for Denver's birth. Although Amy resumes her quest for velvet, she insists that the baby be cognisant of her role. Denver, when she first meets Paul D, is reproved by her mother for calling him 'Mr D' (p. 11). When she meets him in the last section of the book, she calls him Mr D once again (p. 266), exercising her independence and new maturity.

The issue of naming illustrates Morrison's fundamental worries about language. Names can be appropriated and used to impose ideologies and identities, just as language can be manipulated according to the codes of the user and the reader.

THE MOTHER FIGURE

Woman's maternal role is central. The African view is that all mothers are symbols of the marvellous creativity of the earth, but paradoxically, black slave women were rarely able to fulfil this stereotype, actively prevented by the exigencies of slave life. This is historically attested by Sojourner Truth's famous 'Ain't I a woman' speech (1852) in which she asserted the experience of black motherhood as a loss:

> I have borne thirteen children and seen most all sold into slavery and when I cried out a mother's grief, none but Jesus heard me. (C. Boyce Davis, *Black Women Writing and Identity*)

Sethe was suckled by another woman (p. 203), slept apart from her mother, and recognised her by the hat she wore while working and the mark she bore on her ribs (p. 61). Although Sethe's mother claimed her daughter by naming her, in the penultimate section of the novel, we hear Sethe's feelings of pain and resentment enunciated, as Sethe tells Paul D that 'her ma'am' had hurt her feelings (p. 272). She is determined to get her milk to her baby daughter because she has experienced the sensation of being denied the sustenance that was her right.

Baby Suggs is prevented by the system of slavery and persecution from living out her life as a mother. She is denied the possibility of knowing her children as adults, and, by the time of Halle's birth, has given up hope (p. 23) of ever being able to keep her children near her. She accepts the fact that her children are destined to be pawns in a game of checkers instigated, controlled and played by white people. Sethe rebels against these values, that inhibited the black mother's capacity to love, and indulges in a 'thick' love, which results in her violent act in the woodshed. The value vested in a female slave's capacity to reproduce was often manipulated as a form of resistance and there are records of feigned illness, deliberate miscarriages and self-imposed sterility.

Certain feminist readings of the figure of Beloved herself perceive her to be a figure both for Sethe's murdered daughter and for her African mother, taking evidence from Beloved's memories of the Middle Passage in her **interior monologue**. Beloved's presence prompts Sethe to remember her own mother, and these stories about her matrilineal ancestry represent a way of constructing a sense of self and banishing the horrors of the past. Beloved has lost her mother, just as Sethe was separated from her own mother, and the child on the ship who saw her mother throw herself overboard 'she goes in   they do not push her' (p. 212).

In *Beloved*, milk and breasts are used as a **signifier** for motherhood. Many black women were forced to suckle the children of white women. The way Sethe's rights as a black mother are impinged upon is symbolised by the way in which she is robbed of her milk. When Sethe is half-strangled in the Clearing, the realisation that Beloved's breath smells of new milk (p. 98) identifies her as Sethe's daughter.

Sethe's behaviour in killing her baby daughter can be read as an attempt to reclaim her maternal rights and function. It is an act of protection, of putting her babies into safety, which paradoxically becomes an act of extermination. Several slave mothers committed Sethe's fictional crime, and the text focuses on this historical fact. Toni Morrison herself admits the compulsion: 'to deal with this nurturing instinct that expressed itself as murder' (quoted by C. Boyce Davis). Already in *Sula*, her second novel, Toni Morrison examined the mother's right to kill. Eva sets fire to her son with the intent of 'saving' him. Sethe regards her children as possessions that she has made, and Toni Morrison questions whether this is an appropriate stance.

There is an essential conflict between mothering and being an individual. When Sethe first arrives at 124 Bluestone Road Baby Suggs refers to her as 'the mother' (p. 92). She is defined by her biological role. Sethe allows her children to take precedence over herself. She claims that they are the most important things in her life, and shocks Baby Suggs by telling her that she would not take a breath without them. Sethe would die to protect her Denver (p. 99) and tells the unrelenting Beloved that she would renounce her life in its entirety in order to erase just one of Beloved's tears (p. 242). Sethe's mother love is stifling, and Denver must leave the house before she can become a person in her own right. Exclusive mother love of this nature is not endorsed by the text, and as a motive for Sethe killing her daughter, is neither condoned nor condemned – the **dialogic** style and structure of the text resists a single interpretation. The presence of Paul D liberates Sethe as a character, allowing us to learn of her existence before she was overdetermined by her role as mother. However, the arrival of Beloved as a living embodiment of Sethe's mother love and of the painful past of enslavement refocuses the conflict between Sethe's individuality and the overpowering love of motherhood.

Nevertheless, the final expulsion of Beloved and the return of Paul D promise a new future and reintegration into the community from which Sethe has been exiled. Her last words 'Me? Me?' (p. 273) in response to Paul D's suggestion that she herself is her own best thing, suggest the possibility of an identity other than the self-imposed role of mother.

COMMUNITY AND FAMILY

Toni Morrison has admitted (to Robert Stepto) her 'tendency ... to focus on neighbourhoods and families'. In her three earliest works, women, and in particular trios of women attempt to hold whole families together: for example, Pilate in *Song of Solomon* (1977), together with her daughter Reba and granddaughter Hagar, or Eva the one-legged matriarch in *Sula* (1974). In both these novels, the fathers, like Halle in *Beloved*, are absent. Black families historically adapted and changed in reaction to social, political and economic notions of an oppressive society, and during the period of slavery and the years following it, this was especially so. Her latest novel, *Paradise* (1998), features another alternative society of women.

In *Beloved* Toni Morrison presents a ghastly reworking of the successful trio of women of her former works. The grandmother, Baby Suggs, is dead, and the threesome is composed of a homicidal mother, a matricidal ghostly daughter and the resentful Denver, a trio as ominous as the shadows holding hands that Sethe sees. The family is utterly dysfunctional, deprived of males, and characterised by role-swapping between Sethe and her daughters. Toni Morrison is constantly playing with variants of the nuclear structure while alluding to the existence of something much larger and more powerful.

In *Beloved* every character is significant, and the reader may be impressed as much by pivotal characters as by the blood relations from which they derive a sense of themselves, such as Baby Suggs, dead during the course of the novel, but so vitally portrayed. In *Beloved* all characters contribute to the whole. The thumbnail sketch of Lady Jones (p. 247) is as relevant as the squalid details of Stamp Paid and his wife, or Ella and the 'lowest yet' (p. 256). This refusal to privilege pays homage to the African concept of neighbourhood; kinship and responsibilities override a narrow family structure.

It is exactly this system of family life that slavery denied black people. Until he meets Sethe, Paul D is resigned to a life without 'aunts, cousins, children' (p. 221). He recounts the impression that large families make on him (p. 219). The semblance of a community that he was allowed to experience at Sweet Home is easily destroyed once schoolteacher arrives. After her escape Sethe enjoyed only twenty-eight days of community living, experiencing freed life and 'days of healing, ease and real-talk' (pp. 95, 173). It is this concept of shared responsibility that informs Stamp Paid's altruism, as he helps runaways cross the river, and brings messages and food. His anger is great when he discovers that Paul D has been sleeping at the church (p. 186). The power of the community to nurture and sustain its members can also destroy. For Baby Suggs, being abandoned by her community (p. 177), the lack of compassion and understanding from those whom she has known and helped, contributes to her exhaustion, her renunciation of responsibility and finally her death.

Paul D takes Sethe and Denver out of their isolation and into society when he persuades them to accompany him to the carnival. The three are united with each other and with the community: 'No longer the freaks themselves, they set aside the acutely painful otherness of their condition and blend into the diverse and chaotic circus of humanity', comments one critic, D. Heinze. However, this is only a momentary acceptance. Full reintegration is promised from the point at which Denver resolves to seek help for her mother and makes her difficult re-entry into the world outside 124: she is instrumental in healing the rift between her mother and the black community. She begins to find gifts of food, and, on going to thank the first of her benefactors, hears the single and significant word, 'welcome' (p. 249). It is the community of women, led by Ella, who take it upon themselves to save Sethe, the action one of familial love and concern. Sethe, like Sula, has been a useful scapegoat for the community, but Beloved, the living threat from the past, is recognised by Ella (p. 256) and must be exorcised. *Beloved* commemorates the resources that

allowed slaves, in spite of dehumanising conditions, to love themselves
and each other.

The burden of the past

Part of the novel's interest, horror and beauty lies in the way in which
Sethe and Paul D come to terms with their memories, allowing the reader
to share the pain of their lives. Paul D says to Sethe that together they
have 'more yesterday than anybody. We need some kind of tomorrow' (p.
273). Sethe has already acknowledged this factor: 'Her story was bearable
because it was his as well – to tell, to refine, and to tell again' (p. 99). She
also comments on the impossibility of making plans:

> her brain was not interested in the future. Loaded with the past and hungry
> for more, it left her no room to imagine, let alone plan for, the next day.
>
> (p. 70)

Beloved charts the exorcism of this 'yesterday' in order to facilitate a future
for its protagonists. The character of Beloved is an embodiment of the
past, and her appearance stimulates Denver's maturity. She is forgotten
and the novel comes to a close. Significantly, when Sethe fully realises
that Beloved is her daughter, she goes to work wrapped in a 'timeless
present' (p. 184). She abandons her adult responsibilities towards the
future. She loses her job, spends her life-savings on clothes, and defies
temporality by planting a garden out of season. Sethe feels that she can
jettison the burden of her past since Beloved is back. Unfortunately her
guilt is not so easily absolved, as she is punished by her daughter and by
herself. Only at the close of the novel are we left with a feeling that
Sethe's turbulent past has been put to rest. Up to this point, which only
occurs in the epilogue, the past has had a central role in the novel. It is
characterised as a force, leaping in and out of the narrative: 'to Sethe, the
future was a matter of keeping the past at bay' (p. 42), something that has
to be suppressed with aggression, 'the day's work of beating back the past'
(p. 73). The power of the past is demonstrated by the near constant use
of the present tense. Remembered experience is sufficiently vivid to
overpower the boundaries of time. It is only in the epilogue that Toni
Morrison employs a definitive past tense and the distancing that this
entails.

The significance of memory emphasises the power of the past in the novel. Sethe explains her theories to Denver (p. 36), telling her that nothing ever dies, and that the pictures and images of things remain, independent of the existence and experiences of their protagonists. Sethe refers to her 'rememory' and later uses the word 'disremember' to describe self-willed forgetting (p. 118). These unexpected prefixes startle the reader into an awareness of the importance of remembered events. After all, they form the body of the novel. We are sensitised to the process of buried and suppressed memories and, along with the protagonists, we are involved in the process of excavation.

WATER

The image of water runs through *Beloved*. The Ohio River is the boundary that Sethe identifies between herself and freedom. She has no wish to die 'on the bloody side of the Ohio River' (p. 31). Once she has crossed the river she is free to begin a new life. On seeing the river her waters break 'to join it' (p. 83) and she gives birth to Denver. She drinks water from the river, determined not to die on the 'wrong side' (p. 90). When she arrives at 124 Bluestone Road Baby Suggs washes her in sections, purifying her after the ravages of her old life. In the last part of the book, Paul D offers to wash Sethe (p. 272). It is a deeply **symbolic** gesture, and Toni Morrison emphasises this, as Sethe wonders whether he will repeat Baby Suggs's gestures, thus alluding to the possibility of a new life.

Beloved emerges from the water (p. 50), reborn as an adult. On arrival at 124 Bluestone Road she drinks four cupfuls of water. Sethe remembers her baby's dribbling 'clear spit' on her face (p. 93) and, in retrospect, connects this with the water that Beloved drank (p. 202). When Sethe first sees Beloved her bladder overflows and she experiences an artificial delivery. She herself acknowledges the similarity to her waters breaking at Denver's birth (p. 51). Toni Morrison makes a series of references to rivers, rain, snow and ice throughout the novel.

References to water are paralleled by Toni Morrison's recurring use of two other liquids: milk and blood, both tarnished with negative associations. Sethe's milk is stolen from her. The clabber on Halle's face by the butter churn is symbolic of the way in which their family structure has been soured and ruined by slavery. Beloved's blood soaks the narrative, and her death, occurring after twenty-eight days of freedom, 'the travels of one whole moon' (p. 95) alludes to the flow of the menstrual cycle. Water, on the other hand, is aqua vitae, it symbolises cleanliness and rebirth.

EATING AND HUNGER

Excess of food caused the disapproval amongst the black neighbours, so fostering their disinclination to warn Sethe of the arrival of schoolteacher and the slave-catcher. Sethe's food was also spurned at Baby Suggs's funeral, symbolising the rejection of Sethe herself.

It is the need to eat food that forces Denver out of Bluestone Road and into the world, and it is by gifts of food that Denver is reintegrated into community life. Sethe plans a meal as a tribute, an 'offering' (p. 100) to Paul D at the prospect of their shared life together.

Sethe uses the **metaphor** of hunger to describe her brain's willingness to accept the horrors of the past. Her mind, she says, is like a greedy child who will not refuse food. Beloved is the greedy child of the novel, devouring sugar and, finally, Sethe herself. She can be appeased by hearing tales of Sethe's past: 'It became a way to feed her' (p. 58) and sweet things or news can be relied upon to give her pleasure (p. 74). Denver's relationship with Beloved is also characterised with food imagery. Denver's loneliness before Beloved arrives is a hunger, and being looked at by Beloved is 'food enough to last'. Her desire for knowledge is also described as an intellectual hunger to 'eat up a page' (p. 247).

When Sethe is running away from Sweet Home, she fears that she is going to be discovered by another white man with 'mossy teeth, an appetite' (p. 31), and as she waits for him to appear she imagines herself as a pair of jaws. The word 'appetite' is also used to describe the gaze of the undertaker's son as he watches Sethe having sex with his father as payment for the gravestone (p. 5). Eating is associated with rape in the section where Paul D describes the morning ritual in the prison camp. The prisoners are asked whether they are hungry, to which they may only reply in the affirmative, and so are coerced into fellating the guards (see Critical History – Post-Modern Criticism).

The epilogue refers to 'chewing laughter' that 'swallow[s]' (p. 275). This image of ingestion is present in various parts of the novel. Beloved, when she loses a tooth, recounts her dream of exploding or being swallowed (p. 133), and in Beloved's monologue she hears 'chewing and swallowing and laughter' (p. 212). A Freudian interpretation of this imagery suggests sex and sexual violation. The African women who were brought to America on the slave ships were 'consumed' by the men on board, and as often, by the sea itself since many of those who died were thrown overboard.

Part four

Textual analysis

Text 1 (pages 29–30)

Shivering, Denver approached the house, regarding it, as she always did, as a person rather than a structure. A person that wept, sighed, trembled and fell into fits. Her steps and gaze were the cautious ones of a child approaching a nervous, idle relative (someone dependent but proud). A breastplate of darkness hid all the windows except one. Its dim glow came from Baby Suggs' room. When Denver looked in, she saw her mother on her knees in prayer, which was not unusual. What was unusual (even for a girl who had lived all her life in a house peopled by the living activity of the dead) was that a white dress knelt down next to her mother and had its sleeve around her mother's waist. And it was the tender embrace of the dress sleeve that made Denver remember the details of her birth – that and the thin, whipping snow that she was standing in, like the fruit of common flowers. The dress and her mother together looked like two friendly grown-up women – one (the dress) helping out the other. And the magic of her birth, its miracle in fact, testified to that friendliness as did her own name.

Easily she stepped into the told story that lay before her eyes on the path she followed away from the window. There was only one door to the house and to get to it from the back you had to walk all the way around to the front of 124, past the storeroom, past the cold house, the privy, the shed, on around to the porch. And to get to the part of the story she liked best, she had to start way back: hear the birds in the thick woods, the crunch of leaves underfoot; see her mother making her way up into the hills where no houses were likely to be. How Sethe was walking on two feet meant for standing still. How they were so swollen she could not see her arch or feel her ankles. Her leg shaft ended in a loaf of flesh scalloped by five toenails. But she could not, would not, stop, for when she did the little antelope rammed her with horns and pawed the ground of her womb with impatient hooves. While she was walking, it seemed to graze, quietly – so she walked, on two feet meant, in this sixth month of pregnancy, for standing still. Still, near a kettle; still, at the churn; still, at the tub and ironing board. Milk, sticky and sour on her dress attracted every small flying thing from gnats to grasshoppers. By the time she reached the hill skirt she had long ago stopped waving them off. The clanging in her head, begun as a churchbell heard from a distance, was by then a tight cap of pealing bells around her ears. She sank and had to look down to see whether she was in a hole or kneeling. Nothing was alive but her nipples and the little antelope. Finally, she was horizontal – or must have been because blades of wild onion were scratching her temple and her cheek. Concerned as she was for the life of her children's mother Sethe told Denver, she remembered thinking: 'Well, at least I don't have to take another step.'

Denver sees a dress embracing her mother and this vision prompts the memory of the story of her birth which took place during Sethe's escape from Sweet Home. The story of Denver's birth, in the context of Sethe's escape is remembered in fragments throughout the novel. The fact that she was born at all was both magical and miraculous, and Denver is described as a charmed child by both her mother and Baby Suggs.

The quality of this memory is both aural, visual and tactile. Denver *feels* the 'crunch' of leaves, *hears* the birds and *sees* her mother walking. Although Denver begins as a participant, soon the force of the past allows Sethe's thoughts and voice to invade the narrative. Denver as narrator is set aside to such an extent that her reappearance comes as a surprise. A combination of circumstances prompt Denver's memory. The weather and the vision summon and evoke the story, 'like the fruit of common flowers'. This organic **metaphor** illustrates the way in which the text 'grows', allowing **associative** memories to pattern and structure the novel as a whole.

The tale is a 'told' story, and one familiar and loved by Denver who, as her mother recognises, 'hates anything about Sweet Home' (p. 202) while adoring the story of her own birth. This story is given physicality, just as Denver previously personified the house. She steps into a story that lies before her. She compares her arrival at the house, listing the various structures that she has to pass before she arrives, to the progression of the story. Morrison's own narrative necessitates a slow journey past and through other stories in order to arrive at its centre. Similarly, although stories may be 'told' they are not relegated to a closed past, just as America's story of slavery is neither closed nor fixed. The mixing of narrative voices, and the many points of view are part of a larger scheme that points to the impossibility of a fixed and static view of history.

Morrison uses repetition here as in the rest of the novel. The syntactical proximity of the two contrasting phrases: 'which was not unusual' … 'What was unusual' marks the progression of Denver's thoughts. The repetition of the two phrases prefixed by 'How' mark the beginning of our immersion into the flow of the narrative. The interlacing of the passage with the word 'still', repeated five times, creates a poetic effect. The reader notices the **irony** that for Sethe, being still does not entail stopping work. The phrase 'feet meant for standing still' is repeated, with an additional subclause that mentions her pregnancy.

In a compact phrase 'a house peopled by the living activity of the dead', which describes 124, the **paradox** of the dead 'living' and 'peopling' emphasises the inverted nature of Denver's normality. The reader, introduced to the supernatural in the very first pages of the novel, becomes as accustomed as Denver is to poltergeists and manifestations.

The **zeugma** contained in 'Nothing was alive but her nipples and the little antelope' sends the reader back to the central theme of the theft of Sethe's milk, and to the description of the patches of milk on her dress. The extended metaphor of the antelope and the violent verbs describing its movements, graphically convey Sethe's physical discomfort. Language and imagery can be used to transform pain. The detached description of her 'leg shaft', ending particularly visually in the 'loaf' of her foot, is startling. A similar detachment is shown when Sethe defines herself as her children's mother. The roundabout phrase, and the prioritisation of possession and biological role indicate the extent of Sethe's 'too thick' love for her children. She only exists for her offspring, as she tells Beloved, Denver and Baby Suggs. The strength of her love is evinced by her reaction to schoolteacher's return.

TEXT 2   (PAGES 163–4)

Sethe knew the circle she was making around the room, him, the subject, would remain one. That she could never close in, pin it down for anybody who had to ask. If they didn't get it right off, she could never explain. Because the truth was simple, not a long drawn-out record of flowered shifts, tree cages, selfishness, ankle ropes and wells. Simple: she was squatting in the garden and when she saw them coming and recognised schoolteacher's hat, she heard wings. Little hummingbirds stuck their needle beaks right through her headcloth into her hair and beat their wings. And if she thought anything, it was No. No. Nono. Nonono. Simple. She just flew. Collected every bit of life she had made, all the parts of her that were precious and fine and beautiful and carried, pushed, dragged them through the veil, out, away, over there where no one could hurt them. Over there. Outside this place, where they would be safe. And the hummingbird wings beat on. Sethe paused in her circle again and looked out the window. She remembered when the yard had a fence with a gate that somebody was always latching and unlatching in the time when 124 was busy as a way station. She did not see the whiteboys who pulled it down, yanked up the posts and smashed the gate leaving 124 desolate and exposed at the very hour when everybody stopped dropping by. The shoulder weeds of Bluestone Road were all that came towards the house.

When she got back from the jail house, she was glad the fence was gone. That's where they had hitched their horses – where she saw, floating above the railing as she squatted in the garden, schoolteacher's hat. By the time she faced him, looked him dead in the eye, she had something in her arms that stopped him in his tracks. He took a backward step with each jump of the baby heart until finally there were none.

'I stopped him,' she said, staring at the place where the fence used to be. 'I took and put my babies where they'd be safe.'

The roaring in Paul D's head did not prevent him from hearing the pat she gave to the last word, and it occurred to him that what she wanted for her children was exactly what was missing in 124: safety. Which was the very first message he got the day he walked through the door. He thought he had made it safe, had gotten rid of the danger; beat the shit out of it; run it off the place and showed it and everybody else the difference between a mule and a plow. And because she had not done it before he got there her own self, he thought it was because she could not do it. That she lived with 124 in helpless, apologetic resignation because she had no choice; that minus husbands, sons, mother-in-law, she and her slow-witted daughter had to live there all alone making do. The prickly, mean-eyed Sweet Home girl he knew as Halle's girl was obedient (like Halle), shy (like Halle) and work-crazy (like Halle). He was wrong. This here Sethe was new. The ghost in her house didn't bother her for the very same reason that a room-and-board witch with new shoes was welcome. This here Sethe talked about love like any other woman; talked about baby clothes like any other woman, but what she meant could cleave the bone. This here Sethe talked about safety with a handsaw.

This passage presents Sethe's attempt to explain her actions and Paul D's reaction, and marks a **dénouement**. It occurs in the final section of One and is what prompts Paul D's departure and the unleashing of the battle between Sethe and Beloved that is the subject for Three. It is one of the many flashbacks that compose the narrative.

Morrison's **asyntactic** style contrasts long and short sentences. Some sentences are composed of merely one word: 'No' or 'Simple' while others begin with conjunctions such as 'And' and 'Because'. The word 'simple' is repeated three times as Sethe's memory gains immediacy. Initially the word is confined within a sentence, then it is reiterated followed by a semicolon and a phrase, and then finally confined and isolated in an unconventional sentence formed by one single word.

The **metaphor** of the hummingbirds piercing her headcloth conveys Sethe's sense of frantic panic. The monosyllabic words and the plosives simulate the piercing and beating. On two other occasions Sethe experiences this feeling. When she overhears schoolteacher instructing his nephews to align her animal and human characteristics, her scalp prickles as if it were being pierced with 'fine needles'. The metaphor of the hummingbirds is used with exactly the same wording in Three to describe Sethe's attack on Mr Bodwin. There, as in this passage, she 'flew' to protect her children. This choice of verb obviously gains meaning from the preceding metaphor of the hummingbirds.

The repetition of Sethe's negative signals the absolute refutation of events. The single, double and triple 'no' turns an unequivocal denial into a chant, effectively translating Sethe's denial into threatening sound. This visually startling section is followed by a long sentence. Morrison uses three adjectives and three verbs with similar meaning, 'precious, fine ... beautiful ... carried, pushed, dragged ...' followed by a stream of prepositions: 'out, away, over there ... over there ... outside.' This intense passage shows Morrison layering meaning upon meaning, emphasising the extremes of Sethe's love, her activity and her overpowering desire for distance between her children and schoolteacher and the system that he represents.

The same technique is used in the description of the destroyed fence that was 'pulled down ... yanked ... smashed' by white boys, leaving 124 'desolate ... exposed ... everyone stopped dropping by'. We learn that the only visitors to 124 are the plants and are reminded of the first section and the way that people hurry their horses past the house, or that at Baby Suggs's funeral nobody would enter the house. Sethe uses the same verb, 'squatting ... squatted', but, on her second use she adds the new detail of the schoolteacher's hat. In the same way, no related event in the novel is treated as complete, but is continually reworked and refined.

This accumulation of meaning through repetition and the use of **synonyms** is a feature of Morrison's narrative style. It is not confined to her sentence structure but also informs the novel as a whole. On a local level she accumulates verbs or adjectives to give density of meaning, and in the novel, she places account upon account in order to build up the whole, allowing her characters to repeat and echo each other and borrow each other's memories and vocabulary.

In the chilling sentence describing the last beats of her baby's heart, the complicated syntax reflects Sethe's own reluctance to confront the subject. The ordering of the phrases, placing schoolteacher's steps first, then the heartbeats and then their absence faithfully mirrors the course of events. The use of the word 'finally' with its sense of both at last and eventually, can be read as a word imbued with Sethe's feeling. That Sethe should look schoolteacher 'dead', or that her words should 'cleave the bone' demonstrate an appropriate choice of phrase given the context.

Paul D wants to define Sethe in terms of Halle, and the phrase, 'This here Sethe' is repeated, balanced by the bracketed phrase, '(like Halle)'. The repetition emphasises her individuality and the way that she is different from 'any other woman'. As in the rest of the novel, Morrison draws attention to the **multi-accentuality** of words. References to baby clothes, love and safety take on a new dimension when used by Sethe. Sethe defines death as safety, in contradistinction to the danger presented by the system of slavery. As Paul D points out, safety is precisely what is lacking at 124. Sethe's other children cannot be said to have been 'saved' by her actions: Howard and Buglar leave home and may well be dead, while Denver is too afraid to cross the boundaries of the yard. However, as this passage makes clear, Sethe conceives of her children as her own property, as things that she has 'made', and as such, hers to dispense with. The text centres the theme of maternal love and, through its **dialogic** layering of points of view, questions the appropriacy of Sethe's action.

This passage is replete with examples of Morrison's narrative style that echoes Sethe's circling of the subject. Morrison does not 'close … in' or 'pin … down' but adds and evolves, repeating phrases and compacting memory and meaning.

TEXT **3**   (PAGES 225–6)

Sixo is about to crawl out to look for the knives he buried. He hears something. He hears nothing. Forget the knives. Now. The three of them climb up the bank and schoolteacher, his pupils and four other white men move towards them. With lamps. Sixo pushes the Thirty-Mile Woman and she runs further on in the creekbed. Paul D and Sixo run the other way towards the woods. Both are surrounded and tied.

The air gets sweet then. Perfumed by the things honeybees love. Tied like a mule, Paul D feels how dewy and inviting the grass it. He is thinking about that and where Paul D might be when Sixo turns and grabs the mouth of the nearest pointing rifle. He begins to sing. Two others shove Paul D and tie him to a tree. Schoolteacher is saying, 'Alive. Alive. I want him alive.' Sixo swings and cracks the ribs of one, but with bound hands cannot get the weapon in position to use it in any other way. All the whitemen have to do is wait. For his song, perhaps, to end? Five guns are trained on him while they listen. Paul D cannot see them when they step away from lamplight. Finally one of them hits Sixo in the head with his rifle, and, when he comes to, a hickory fire is in front of him and he is tied at the waist to a tree. Schoolteacher has changed his mind: 'This one will never be suitable'. The song must have convinced him.

The fire keeps failing and the whitemen are put out with themselves at not being prepared for this emergency. They came to capture, not kill. What they can manage is only enough for cooking hominy. Dry faggots are scarce and the grass is slick with dew.

By the light of the hominy fire Sixo straightens. He is through with his song. He laughs. A rippling sound like Sethe's sons make when they tumble in hay or splash in rainwater. His feet are cooking, the cloth of his trousers smokes. He laughs. Something is funny. Paul D guesses what it is when Sixo interrupts his laughter to call out: 'Seven-O! Seven-O!'

Smoky, stubborn fire. They shoot him to shut him up. Have to.

Shackled, walking through the perfumed things honeybees love, Paul D hears the men talking and for the first time learns his worth. He has always known, or believed he did, his value – as a hand, a laborer who could make profit on a farm – but now he discovers his worth, which is to say, he learns his price. The dollar value of his weight, his strength, his heart, his brain, his penis, and his future.

This is the botched escape from Sweet Home and Sixo's triumphant death. Sixo's last laugh, mentioned in One, Section 2, is finally **contextualised** here. Laughter is a seditious force in the novel. Baby Suggs laughs when she discovers the beating of her free heart, and her laugh is what finally launches Denver into the yard and out into the community. Similarly Paul D's laughter on the trip to the carnival has the power to begin to thaw the negative feelings that the community harbours against Sethe.

Sixo's woman, Patsy, rebaptised as the Thirty-Mile Woman because of the distance Sixo has to walk to meet her, escapes. The source of Sixo's laughter is that she is pregnant with his baby. The man, whose name derives from a number, has triumphed in spite of his capture and succeeded in the continuation of his lifeline, shouting 'Seven-O! Seven-O!'. In one word he signifies to Paul D the escape of his unborn child and simultaneously names the child after himself. With this one word, Sixo binds himself to his woman, his child, his world and his friend with links infinitely stronger than white men's ropes.

The use of the present tense adds immediacy to the unfolding of the narrative. The sparse sentences: 'He hears something. He hears nothing,' convey the anxiety of the listener, while the strong imperative: 'Forget' and the one word sentence, 'Now.' add to the urgency of the moment. The detached description of the terrible turn of events, and the use of a passive construction, 'Both are surrounded and tied' increases the horrific nature of the scene. Similarly Paul D's observation of the sweetness of the air, a phrase later repeated with a reorganisation of the words: 'perfumed by the things honeybees love … the perfumed things honeybees love' is a further use of distancing. It follows a dramatic section, and effectively slows the narrative down, drawing the reader's attention towards the incongruity of the setting. Paul D's thoughts, his aesthetic observations, and his rhetorical question that the men are waiting, 'For his song, perhaps, to end?' create an eerie effect for the reader, who cannot help but be transfixed by the development of events.

Sixo's song has the power to delay death and to extinguish the fire, whilst ensuring his end. Schoolteacher refers to him as 'this one', and the anonymity of the phrase demonstrates the little importance Sixo has as a human being. The **alliterative** failing fire prompts a pun. The men themselves are 'put out', and the phrase 'hominy fire' is full of implicit scorn.

The 'smoky stubborn fire' necessitates the shooting of Sixo. The continued alliteration and the **assonance** of 'shoot ... shut' introduces an element of linguistic play into the narrative, just as the comparison of Sixo's laughter to Sethe's baby sons, or the sweet air distracts the reader. The ominous and self-justifying 'Have to', enunciated from the whiteman's perspective, concludes the episode.

Paul D is tied and shackled like a beast and overhears white men talking about him. The agglomeration of economic terms: 'worth ... value ... profit ... worth ... price ... dollar value' underlines Paul D's status as a piece of property. Here we see Morrison's customary interest in the **polysemous** nature of language. Paul D thinks of his own 'value' in terms of work, but realises his 'dollar value' is something quite different. His worth is equated with his price and not what he is able to do or offer. Worth is not an abstract noun, denoting qualities, but a noun linked to a fixed monetary sum. The listing of Paul D's physical, reproductive and intellectual powers in relation to their price is dehumanising, showing the way in which an individual can be perceived only in terms of parts. The message of slavery, which bases itself on this perception, is in direct contrast to Baby Suggs's exhortations in the Clearing to love and assimilate those single parts.

PART FIVE

BACKGROUND

TONI MORRISON AND HER LITERARY WORKS

Toni Morrison, a black American, was born Chloe Anthony Wofford, on 18 February 1931, the second of four children, in Lorain, Ohio. She grew up during the Depression. Both sets of her grandparents had moved north from the South. Her father, George Wofford, was originally from Georgia and knew the reality of racial violence. He worked as a welder in a shipyard, holding three jobs simultaneously for seventeen years, and was sufficiently proud of his workmanship for him to engrave his name in the side of the ship whenever he welded a perfect seam. Her mother, Ramah Willis Wofford, was a similarly strong-minded parent; when the family was on relief she wrote a long letter to Franklin Roosevelt complaining about the fact that they received insect-ridden grain. She took 'humiliating jobs' (as Toni Morrison would reveal in an interview with Nellie McKay) in order to finance her daughter's education. Toni Morrison recalls that her parents disagreed about 'whether it was possible for white people to improve'. Her father thought that it was not, while her mother was more optimistic, believing that whites might surprise them with their humanity. Despite this difference of opinion they both relied on their black friends and family, and, as Susan Blake relates in Morrison's own words, taught their children that 'all succour and aid came from themselves and their neighbourhood'.

Toni Morrison grew up in an environment steeped in black culture, ritual, music and language, in a family that encouraged her to believe in herself and be proud of her origins.

When she entered first grade at school, Chloe was the only black child in the class, and the only child who knew how to read. As an adolescent she read the great classics avidly – works by Jane Austen, Flaubert and the major Russian novelists – somewhat in awe of their grand style and their attention to detail. She graduated with honours from Lorain High School and went on to Howard University, where she studied English and Classics. It was here that she adopted the name Toni, because people found the pronunciation of Chloe difficult.

She joined the university drama group and took plays on tour in the South. Her travels there were a revelation to her, and a similar journey figures in her third novel, *Song of Solomon*.

In 1955 she received a master's degree in English from Cornell University. Her thesis was on the theme of suicide in the works of William Faulkner and Virginia Woolf. After this she taught at Texas Southern University for two years and returned to Howard in 1957 as an English teacher.

There she met and married her husband, Harold Morrison, a Jamaican architect, and began her writing career. She refuses to talk about her marriage which ended in 1964, when she returned to her parents' house with her two small sons.

She then became a senior editor for the publisher Random House, and commissioned autobiographies by Mohammed Ali and Angela Davis, as well as publishing fiction by Toni Cade Bambara, Henry Dumas and Gayl Jones. Her aims as an editor reflect her purpose as a writer: 'I look very hard for black fiction because I want to participate in developing a canon of black work ... black people talking to black people' (S. Blake). In the early 1970s she began to write for newspapers and literary journals, in particular the *New York Times*, where, between 1971 and 1972 she reviewed twenty-eight books about black life, and wrote articles about black life itself, including a piece entitled 'What the Black Woman thinks about Women's Lib'. She explained her career trajectory to Nellie McKay: 'All my work has to do with books. I teach books, write books, edit books, or talk about books. It is all one thing.'

If all her work can be traced to an interest in books, it is also unified by a passion for black history and issues of black identity. She has an academic and personal interest in race. She taught African-American literature and creative writing at SUNY/Purchase, Yale University. Her first critical publication, *Playing in the Dark* (1992), appearing simultaneously with her sixth novel, *Jazz*, is a probing enquiry into the significance of African Americans in the American literary imagination. She examines the work of Willa Cather, Poe, Hawthorne and Melville and the dark presence within their writing. She has also edited and co-edited two works of cultural criticism that deal with high-profile events in America: *Race-ing Justice, En-gendering Power: Essays on Anita Hill, Clarence Thomas and the Construction of Social Reality* (1993) and, together with Claudia Brodsky Lacour, Morrison edited *Birth of a Nation'Hood: Gaze, Script and Spectacle in the O.J.Simpson Case* (1997).

Toni Morrison holds an unusual position within the ranks of black female writers, a group usually restricted to the fringe of the literary establishment. She has had amazing success in her life and work, and has received national and international acclaim. After *Song of Solomon* was published in 1977 it became a bestseller and won the prestigious National Book Critic's Circle Award for fiction in 1978. She has received an American Academy and Institute of Arts and Letters Award and featured in the PBS series of Writers in America. In 1980 she was appointed by President Carter to the National Council on the Arts, and in 1981 she was elected to the American Academy and Institute of Arts and Letters. In 1988 she won the Pulitzer Prize. In 1993 she was awarded the ultimate accolade, the Nobel Prize for Literature – the first time that this award had been given to an African American. Currently she is the Robert F. Gohoen Professor, Council of Humanities, at Princeton University. Her readership is wide-ranging: the appeal of her work crosses racial, cultural and class boundaries. Her novels are studied for their insights into both black culture and feminist theories, and are enthusiastically read by black and white readers alike.

Besides *Beloved*, which was published in 1987, she has written six other novels: *The Bluest Eye* (1970), *Sula* (1974), *Song of Solomon* (1977), *Tar Baby* (1981), *Jazz* (1992) and *Paradise* (1998). Their settings and themes gradually broaden. Her first novel focuses on young girls and the damaging effect of stereotypical white ideals of beauty, while her second novel deals with the theme of friendship between women. *In Song of Solomon* she extends her focus to include not only black women but a black man, Milkman Dead, in search of his identity. By the time of the writing of *Tar Baby* in 1981, a novel set in the Caribbean, New York and Florida, she is dealing with both men and women, black and white and their respective roles in contemporary society. *Beloved, Jazz* and *Paradise* were conceived as a trilogy, each chronicling black women's search for a sense of self. For this reason in particular it is ill-advised to isolate *Beloved* from Morrison's other works, but nevertheless *Beloved* is the text that has sealed Morrison's reputation and has generated most discussion and literary criticism to date. *Beloved* has had spectacular acclaim for its intense and extraordinary features. It has been described as: 'a stunning book and lasting achievement [which] transforms the sorrows of history into the luminous truth of art' (M. Rubin in *Christian Science Monitor*). It has also been hailed as: 'a milestone in the chronicling of the black experience in America' (*Publishers' Weekly*).

Toni Morrison is now famous, and rightly so, for her mysterious blend of realism and fantasy, which is rooted in black folklore and her family's tradition of story-telling. She evokes place and culture with all the specificity of the writers she admired as a teenager, but place and culture of an utterly different kind – that of America's black underclass. In her writing as in her life, she is an anomaly, combining the highest professional success with a background of poverty and racism, appealing to both the general public and academics, and obtaining the success that many black female writers have been denied.

LITERARY BACKGROUND

The context for Toni Morrison and her work is clearly linked to her race and gender. She herself identifies a black style, an 'ineffable quality that is curiously black' (Nellie McKay) and her work is steeped in popular black culture, its music and folklore. Her novels juxtapose and combine joy and pain, laughter and tears and love and death. These same combinations are the essence of blues, jazz and spirituals, and were the themes exploited by story-tellers. The tradition of black female writers to which Morrison belongs is a similarly strong factor in her work. The first black published writers in America were female slaves: for example Phyllis Wheatley who wrote *Poems on Various Subjects, Religious and Moral* (1773) or Lucy Terry, author of *Bars Fight* (1746). The literary movement of the 1920s, known as the Harlem Renaissance, had several female protagonists, most notably Jessie Fausset who produced four novels between 1924 and 1933, while the character of Janie in Zora Neale Thurston's *Their Eyes were Watching God* (1937) heralds the advent of the black feminist heroine to American literature. In the 1970s the Women's Rights Movement and the Black Rights Movement intersected, and black women began to write about their experiences with a strong sense of autobiography and of female history, as can been seen in the works of Maya Angelou or Alice Walker. The existence of authoritarian and creative grandmother and mother figures – very true in Morrison's own case – have given rise to a conception of black female writing as a dialogue with the women of the past.

In terms of genre, Morrison's *Beloved* can be seen as having significantly different emphases from the slave narratives of the nineteenth century, a body of works almost 6,000 in number. These narratives contain a longing for freedom and self-respect while chronicling the slaves' life on the plantations, their suffering and eventual escape. Two examples of the genre are: *The Narrative of Frederick Douglass, An American Slave* (1847) and Harriet Jacob's *Incidents in the Life of a Slave Girl* (1861). *Beloved* is not a personal account of slavery, it also encompasses the fate of all the inhabitants of Sweet Home and of various other protagonists besides Sethe. It is a composite story of slaves and their quest for freedom. However, she subverts the tradition of the slave narrative in various ways. Although the subject matter is the same, her purpose is very different. The slaves of the nineteenth century wrote with an explicit intent to effect the abolition of slavery, had to limit their stories for fear of offending the sensibilities of their white readers who alone could be responsible for ending slavery. Even the immediate pain of their memories was curtailed in their accounts, rather like Sethe, who skimps on details in her replies to Denver's questions about her past, and is successful in almost entirely blocking out the first thirteen years of her life.

Writing in the twentieth century, Toni Morrison's purpose is still a corrective one: the history of slavery must not be forgotten. Her purpose is to 'fill in the blanks that the traditional slave narrative left', as she explains in her essay 'The Site of Memory'. She chronicles the psychological damage slavery inflicted on men in the figures of Paul D and Halle. However, she concentrates on an elaboration of female pain, the history that is inscribed in the mental and physical scars that each woman in her narrative bears. The pain of not knowing one's children, of losing husbands and being continually at risk of sexual exploitation.

Black women can reclaim their history by writing about it, and the style of *Beloved*, which pays tribute to the non-literary background of black culture, places the novel at the very heart of this process. Toni

Morrison uses different protagonists' varying visions of events to compile her history of slavery, and this can been seen as part of a contemporary trend to see history as multiple and inconclusive. There are significant gaps in her narrative: the past is not divided from the present, the two are interdependent and the boundaries between them are blurred. This is very different from the precision of history books, with their attention to prominent figures and the treatment of facts as fixed entities. It is possible to view *Beloved* as a 'history of the present', where the consequences of slavery's brutality are examined through the 'rememory' of her characters.

HISTORICAL BACKGROUND

Beloved begins in 1873, though the narrative stretches back to include memories of Sethe's mother, and Baby Suggs (Sethe's mother-in-law). Toni Morrison focuses on the issue of slavery by fictionalising the historical fact that slave mothers sometimes killed their children rather than allow them to become slaves. Such an event is recounted in the story of Margaret Garner, which appears in *The Black Book* (see Bibliography p. 72), a work conceived by Morrison and made up of newspaper cuttings, songs, photographs, recipes and other memorabilia, to produce a history of anonymous black men and women. Like Garner, Sethe kills her daughter and attempts to destroy her other children to prevent them from being recaptured as fugitives. Morrison says she wrote *Beloved* convinced that:

> this has got to be the least read of all the books I'd written because it is about something that the characters don't want to remember, I don't want to remember, black people don't want to remember, white people don't want to remember. I mean, it's national amnesia. (B. Angelo, 'The Pain of Being Black')

A regular slave trade between Africa and the English North American colonies began in the early seventeenth century. Merchant shippers of New York and New England imported slaves as regular merchandise for the planters of Maryland, Virginia and the Carolinas. By 1670 both law and custom defined all Africans in the colonies as slaves. By 1776 the colonies had a slave population of more than 50,000, the majority based south of Maryland. The slave system began to come under criticism in the eighteenth century. Antislavery societies were founded in England in 1787 and in France in 1788 – but their efforts met with little support in America. After the invention of the cotton gin (a machine that separates the seeds and hulls from cotton fibre) in 1793, the subsequent boom in the production of cotton created a greater demand for slaves. While the transatlantic trade diminished, slave owners took to breeding their own slaves. Some states, for example Virginia in 1832, were so successful in this enterprise that they were able to export as many as 6,000 slaves. Organised merchant firms and slave markets were established. Despite the legal cessation of the slave trade after 1808, slaves continued to be imported from Africa. By 1860, the American slave population numbered well over 3 million. During the nineteenth century, the institution came under attack from religious groups and from secular politicians with humanitarian motives.

In America, the problem of slavery was a provocative political issue between the pro-abolitionist North and the pro-slavery South, especially over the question of refugee slaves. The Supreme Court Decision of 1857 appeared to give slavery new legal support and set the stage for the Civil War that raged between northern and southern states in America from 1861 to 1865. The Union forces of the North won the war in 1865 and the Thirteenth Amendment in the Constitution (1865) abolished slavery in the United States. There were, however, other more complex reasons for the Civil War, slavery being only a small part. However these are beyond the scope of this Note.

Even after the end of the war, persecution and injustice were still very much part of black people's lives. As Stamp Paid reflects (in 1874): 'whole towns wiped clean of Negroes; eighty-seven lynchings in one year alone in Kentucky; four colored schools burnt to the ground: grown men whipped like children, children whipped like adults, black women raped …' (p. 180).

After the Thirteenth Amendment the North imposed Reconstruction – a period of racial readjustment – on the South that lasted from 1865 to 1877. Four million emancipated blacks were granted the social and legal rights that Southern whites had felt to be their own. As a response the KKK (Ku Klux Klan) was formed in 1866. The end of Reconstruction inaugurated a political climate of fear for black people in the States. Between 1882 and 1903 over 2,000 black people were lynched. The attitudes that had allowed slavery to exist resurfaced in the opposition to the Civil Rights Movements of the 1950s and persist to this day in extremist right-wing groups and racist attacks.

James Baldwin (1924–87) a famous black writer and social activist, writes in *Notes of a Native Son* (1955) that 'The past is all that makes the present coherent'. History plays a crucial role in shaping identity, both black and white. The history of slavery is personally significant for Morrison and for all black and white people. The past must not be neglected or forgotten, and Morrison sets herself against the 'national amnesia' she perceives as surrounding the issue of slavery. For Morrison, black history is the core of black identity. As Susan Blake has pointed out, it is not a case of 'forging new myths' but of 're-discovering the old ones'. In this process lies the clue not only to 'the way we really were' but to 'the way we really are'.

PART SIX

CRITICAL HISTORY AND BROADER PERSPECTIVES

Beloved is a novel that has generated great critical attention due to both its content and form. Over 400 articles have been written about Morrison since its publication, and over a third of these deal with that text in particular. Morrison has acquired **canonical** status herself and through this acquisition has the power to question ideas about canonicity. Her significance as an African-American cultural figure cannot be underestimated.

The reader should beware of **tokenism** and of the politics inherent in reading. It is obvious that the most that this Note can do is to point the reader towards the critical works that deal in greater depth with the various readings of *Beloved*. The works cited represent different trends, but are by no means an exhaustive bibliography. A very good critical introduction to *Beloved*, which has the advantage of citing several key articles and positions, is the Icon Critical Guide, edited by Carl Plasa, Icon, 1998.

Morrison helps the reader to comprehend her narrative strategy, through her own critical comments given in many interviews. See in particular Danille Taylor-Guthrie, *Conversations with Toni Morrison* (Roundhouse Publications, 1994). Morrison's work contains so many elements that many different readings exist. Often they are difficult to separate from each other. Feminist readings automatically focus on questions of race, just as readings that place Morrison in the context of African-American literary tradition also dwell on her position as a female writer.

AFRICAN-AMERICAN WRITING

For the **intertextual** relationship between *Beloved* and the slave narrative genre see Literary Background. For an overview of the genre, *The Slave's Narrative*, ed. Henry Louis Gates Jnr and Charles T. Davis is recommended. Morrison herself discusses her position in 'The Site of

Memory', which was originally given as a lecture and then later published in 'Inventing the Truth: The Art and Craft of Memoir' (1987), ed. William Zissner. She comments on the denial of 'interior life' in these texts, and their inevitable reluctance (determined by their enfranchised white readership) to reveal fully the terrible psychological and physical damage inflicted by slavery. Both of these factors are redressed through the use of memory in *Beloved*. The subject of Morrison's relationship to the slave narratives is examined in depth by Marilyn Saunders Mobley. The slave narratives were largely delivered using the first person and tended to develop sequentially. In contrast, *Beloved* is **dialogic**, the treatment of time is quite the opposite from **linear narrative**, and memory and the psychological effects of slavery and interior life have more weight than the historical fact, which is introduced largely through the memories of Paul D. Moreover, the 'veil' which Morrison feels was drawn too often on the horrific experiences is torn down as she foregrounds the female black slave's experience.

Beloved is **contextualised** in the genre of African-American women's historical writings by Barbara Christian, in her essay, 'Somebody Forgot to Tell Somebody Something' which analyses the treatment of slavery in the literature of the last two centuries, but examines why black women's historical novels should be appearing now. Gina Wisker places a reading of *Beloved* and Alice Walker's *The Temple of My Familiar* as products of 'Black, female, folk-culture' (p. 87) and Boyce Davis compares Sherley Anne William's *Dessa Rose* (1986) with *Beloved* (as have Kirsten Holmes, *Literature Interpretation Theory*, no.6, 1995, and Anne E. Goldman, *Feminist Studies*, no.16, 1990). Mbalia places Morrison within the African-American tradition, and examines all her novels in terms of Morrison's developing commitment to share the struggle for a solution to the problems facing African people.

According to Holloway and Demetrakopoulos in *New Dimensions of Spirituality*, much of Morrison's work manifests 'a celebration of African archetypes'. The most significant is the Great Mother, the giver of life and wisdom, who is *nommo*, the creative and sacred actualisation of nature. Like nature, the Great Mother can kill as well as create. R.G. Schmidt has examined the aspects of *nommo* in *Beloved* and particularly the importance of hearing, calling and naming in the text. This essay can be found at http://www.afrinet.net. Harris explores the importance of the black oral tradition which places Morrison's work within the African-American tradition. She argues the case for Morrison's novels as 'speakerly texts' or 'talking books' that unite form and content through the use of story-telling materials.

Linden Peach has formulated a distinction between 'syncretist' and 'separatist' criticism of African-American literature. The first requires that African-American writing be placed within a specifically African cultural context. This approach is often associated with a certain reluctance to use literary theory since it is perceived as part and parcel of the racial domination which black writing tries to eliminate. Barbara Christian feels that Western critical methods do not deal with *Beloved*'s concern with 'African belief systems'. In contrast, those who support the syncretist mode believe that African-American writing benefits from being examined as a hybrid cultural form.

Some useful texts include:

B. Christian, '"Somebody Forgot to Tell Somebody Something" African-American Women's Historical Novels', in J.M. Braxton and A.N. McLaughin, eds, *Wild Women in the Whirlwind: Afra-American Culture and the Contemporary Literary Renaissance*, Rutgers University Press, 1990

– 'Fixing Methodologies: *Beloved*', *Cultural Critique 24*, Spring 1993

H.L. Gates, C.T. Davis, *The Slave's Narrative*, Oxford University Press, 1985

K.F.C. Holloway, Stephanie Demetrakopoulous, *New Dimensions of Spirituality*, Greenwood Press, 1987

T. Harris, *Fiction and Folklore: The novels of Toni Morrison*, Ohio State University Press, 1991

M.S. Mobley, 'A Different Remembering: Memory, History and Meaning in Toni Morrison's *Beloved*, Harold Bloom, ed., *Toni Morrison*, Chelsea House, 1990
> The essay is also cited almost in its entirety in the Icon Critical Guide to *Beloved*, edited by Carl Plasa, and published in 1998

Dorothea D. Mbalia, *Toni Morrison's Developing Class Consciousness*, Associated University Presses, 1991

L. Peach, *Toni Morrison*, Macmillan, 1995

G. Wisker, ed., *Black Women's Writing*, Macmillan, 1993

FEMINIST CRITICISM

The way in which Morrison has written a 'her'-story, prioritising the voice of Sethe, a black female slave, and her search through narrative and memory of a sense of self is a subject for many feminist studies. Women's roles: in the underground railroad, in African spirituality and in subverting slavery are developed in *Beloved*. Denise Heinze uses W.E. DuBois's term of double consciousness in her examination of Morrison's paradoxical role as a black female 'minority' writer who is read by Americans of all classes and races. The way in which the female body is written upon, the scars on Sethe's back that are inscribed by schoolmaster's nephews and renamed by Amy and Paul D are examined as a way of figuring male and white discourse on a female black subject. This is treated in depth in an article by Mae G. Henderson, who uses theories from historiography and psychoanalysis in her examination of memory and the past in *Beloved*. She discusses the symbolism of the ink that Sethe makes which is used by schoolteacher. Marks and signs have also been examined by Carole Boyce Davis in *Black Women, Writing, Identity and the Subject* and in her reading of Sethe as a 'concentration of female identity' (p. 138). The significance of the mother/daughter relationship is treated by almost all critics in more or less detail. Marianne Hirsch argues that, in *Beloved*, Morrison has 'opened the space for maternal narrative in feminist fiction'. For an exclusively feminist theoretical reading of *Beloved* Barbara Hill Rigney examines Morrison's treatment of maternal space, her radical use of language and her interpretations of history as both fact and mythology. She suggests that the fragmentary narrative style of Two, Section 4 is determined by the painful subject matter, and supports her theory that 'rememory' is an example of 'psychic racial memory' since Beloved, who has never been a slave and died aged two, nevertheless has inherited the memories of the slave ships and the Middle Passage.

Some feminist readings of *Beloved* include:

C. Boyce Davis, *Black Women, Writing, Identity and the Subject*, Routledge, 1994

H. Carby, *Reconstructing Womanhood – The Emergence of the Afro-American Woman Novelist*, Oxford University Press, 1995

D. Heinze, *The Dilemma of 'Double Consciousness' – Toni Morrison's Novels*, University of Georgia Press, 1993

M.G. Henderson, 'Toni Morrison's *Beloved*: Re-membering the Body as Historical Text', in H.J. Spillers, ed., *Comparative American Identities: Race, Sex and Nationality in the Modern Text*, Routledge, 1991

B. Hill Rigney, *The Voice of Toni Morrison*, Ohio State University Press, 1991

Marianne Hirsch, *The Mother/Daughter Plot: Narrative, Psychoanalysis, Feminism*, Indiana University Press, 1989

PSYCHOANALYTIC CRITICISM

Morrison's use of 'rememory' and the figure of Beloved herself have given rise to many psychoanalytical readings of the text. Desire drives *Beloved*, since the women at 124 can be seen to have willed Beloved into existence. Thus Freud's concept of 'the return of the repressed' has obvious resonance for *Beloved*. Freud developed the theory of psychoanalysis as a means of curing neuroses in his patients, but its concepts were expanded by him and his followers as a means of understanding human behaviour and culture generally. Nicholls uses the Freudian concept of *Nachtraglichkeit*, or deferred action, as a way of dealing with traumatic experience in his treatment of *Beloved*, examining the way in which this is used in the local detail of the writing and in the novel as a whole. The way in which character's references gain resonance are explained in the light of later references, a phenomenon described by Nicholls as 'retroactive effect', see for example the early reference to Sixo's laugh, or Sethe's reference to the bit (p. 58) which the reader later links with her mother and with Paul D. Sethe's refusal to mourn her dead daughter is examined in the light of other psychoanalytic theories.

Denise Heinze reads Beloved as a psychological phenomenon, perceiving her as Sethe's double, and that her development – from baby to murderous adult – reflects the development of Sethe's own life. This view naturally changes the implications of Beloved's seduction of Paul D. In this reading Beloved is also perceived as 'the projection of repressed collective memory of a violated people' (p. 179). The readings of the flesh-and-blood Beloved as a baby stranded at the stage of primary identification with her mother derive much from psychoanalytical theories of child development.

Some psychoanalytic readings include:

J. Fitzgerald, 'Selfhood and Community: Psychoanalysis and Discourse in *Beloved*', *Modern Fiction Studies*, 39, 1993

D. Heinze, *The Dilemma of 'Double Consciousness' – Toni Morrison's Novels* op.cit.

P. Nicholls, 'The Belated Postmodern: History, Phantoms and Toni Morrison', *Psychoanalytic Criticism: A Reader*, ed. Sue Vice, Polity Press, 1995

J. Wyatt, 'Giving Body to the Word: The Maternal Symbolic in Toni Morrison's *Beloved*', *PMLA 108*, 1993

POST-MODERN CRITICISM

Post-modernism is a convenient if bewildering blanket term with which to describe many different ways of reading. The very fact of having a **dialogic** narrative underlines the fact that various interpretations can exist of the same events. The contradictory and fragmented version of history put forward in *Beloved*, and the denial of crucial information, for example whether and when Halle died, or Beloved's name and nature, undermine the reader's sense of security. The figure of Beloved herself is intrinsically post-modern since she is two things simultaneously, both Sethe's daughter returned from the dead and an embodiment of the tragic past of slavery.

The body is given relevance in *Beloved*, whether through the negative appropriation of the milk from Sethe's breasts or the various kinds of rape figured in the text (see Pamela Barnett, 'Figurations of Rape and the Supernatural in *Beloved*), or the movements of the chai... or through Baby Suggs's positive evocation to love the body and its organs (see April Lidinsky, 'Prophesying Bodies: Calling for a Politics of Collectivity in Toni Morrison's Beloved' in *Discourse of Slavery: Aphra Behn to Toni Morrison*, eds Carl Plasa and Betty J. Ring, Routledge, 1994). This is material for post-structuralist and post-modernist theorising about the capacity of language to construct subjectivity. Paul D's own questions about the nature of his identity, whether Garner was 'naming what he saw, or creating what he did not' (p. 220) are questions that these critics unravel. Many of the critical works cited below take for granted *Beloved*'s status as a post-modern text.

OTHER BOOKS AND ARTICLES REFERRED TO IN THE TEXT

B. Angelo, 'The Pain of Being Black', *Time*, 22 May 1989

S. Blake, 'Toni Morrison', from T. Harris, T. Davis, eds, *Afro-American Writers After 1955, The Dictionary of Literary Biography Vol. 33*, Gale Research, 1984

'The Looting of Language', *The Guardian*, 9 December 1993

A. Lidinsky, Review of *Beloved*, *Publisher's Weekly*, 17 July 1987

N. McKay, 'An Interview with Toni Morrison', *Contemporary Literature 24*, Winter 1983, pp. 413–29

T. Morrison, H. Middleton, eds, *The Black Book*, Random House, 1974

T. Morrison, *Playing in the Dark, Whiteness and the Literary Imagination*, Picador, 1983

– *Lecture and Speech of Acceptance, upon the award of the Nobel Prize for Literature*, Knopf, 1994

M. Rubin, Review of *Beloved*, *Christian Science Monitor*, 5 October 1987

M. Saunders Mobley, 'The Mellow Moods and Difficult Truths of Toni Morrison', *The Southern Review*, Summer 1993

C. Tate, 'A Conversation with Toni Morrison', *Black Women Writers at Work*, Continuum, 1983

D. Taylor-Guthrie, ed., *Conversations with Toni Morrison*, Roundhouse Publications, 1994

1835	Halle and Sethe born
1848	Sethe comes to Sweet Home, aged 13, to replace Baby Suggs who was freed, 'a sixty-odd year old' (p. 141)
1849	Sethe and Halle get married, and enjoy 'six whole years of marriage' (p. 23)
1850-2	Howard and Buglar born
1853	First daughter (Beloved?) born
1855	Sethe's escape from Sweet Home. Denver's premature birth at six months. Halle's death (?). Baby Suggs claims to have felt him die on day that Denver was born (p. 8)
1856	Paul D in prison camp in Alfred
1862	Denver, aged 7, goes to school for a year and becomes deaf in order not to confront her mother's past
c1865	Baby Suggs's death. Denver's hearing returns. Howard and Buglar leave
1869	Paul D in Rochester
1873 one	Paul D's arrival. Beloved's appearance
1874 two	'Eighteen seventy-four and white folks were still on the loose' (p. 180)
1875 three	*April.* Denver leaves the house to seek help; by *June* has learnt 52 pages of Bible verse (p. 250); *summer* Beloved's exorcism

Events	Author's life	Literary world
1619 Beginning of Slave Trade to Virginia		
1640s Sugar cultivation begins, West Indies		
1680s Royal African Company exporting 5,000 slaves per annum		
		1746 Lucy Terry, *Bars Fight*
		1773 Phyllis Wheatley, *Poems on Various Subjects, Religious and Moral*
1775-83 5,000 blacks fight in American Revolution		
1780s Britain exporting 74,000 slaves per annum		
1793 Invention of Cotton Gin		
1800 Gabriel Prosser leads slave insurrection, Virginia		
1807 Britain outlaws slave trade but it persists in Southern States of America		
1820s Evangelical revival in North America leads to Abolitionist movement		
1821 Harriet Tubman, slave, born – later 'conductor' on 'underground railroad'		
1830 2 million black slaves in US		
1831 Nat Turner hanged after leading slave revolt, Virginia		**1831** William Lloyd Garrison founds *Liberation*
1833 Slavery abolished in British Empire; foundation of The American Anti-Slavery Society		**1833-40** Abolitionist writings by John Greenleaf Whittier
1840 World Anti-Slavery Convention, London; Wendell Phillips, delegate		
		1847 *The Narrative of Frederick Douglass, An American Slave*

Events	Author's life	Literary world
		1852 Harriet Beecher Stowe, *Uncle Tom's Cabin*
1859 John Brown, abolitionist, hanged after capture of Harper's Ferry arsenal and recapture by Robert E. Lee		
1861-5 American Civil War		1861 Harriet Jacob, *Incidents in the Life of a Slave Girl*
1863 Abraham Lincoln's Emancipation Proclamation frees almost 4 million slaves		
1865 Amendment to US constitution prohibits slavery; Lincoln assassinated		
1875 Tennessee passes segregationist laws		
1890s Jazz evolves from black spirituals and worksongs		
1896 Supreme Court upholds separate but equal treatment for blacks		
1910 National Association for Advancement of Colored Peoples founded		
		1912 James Weldon Johnson, *Autobiography of an Ex-Colored Man*
1914 Marcus Garvey founds Universal Negro Improvement Association for worldwide unity among blacks		
1914-18 First World War		
		1917 Gwendolyn Brooks, first black writer to win Pulitzer Prize
1920s The Jazz Age		1920s-30s Harlem Renaissance; W.E.B. Bois's *Crisis* magazine
		1922 Claude McKay, *Harlem Shadows*
		1923 Jean Toomer, *Cane*
		1924-33 4 novels by Jessie Fausset
		1925 Countee Cullen, *Color*
1926 Paul Robeson tours US singing spirituals		1926 Langston Hughes, *The Weary Blues*

Events	Author's life	Literary world
1928 Robeson sings 'Ol' Man River' in *Showboat*		
1930 Black Muslims founded		**1930s-40s** Flourishing of *Négritude* movement under Léopold Senghor
	1931 Birth of **Chloe (Toni) Anthony Wofford** in Lorain, Ohio, daughter of a welder	**1931** Arna Bontemps, *God Sends Sunday*
1936 J.C. Owens wins 4 Olympic golds, Berlin		**1936** Arna Bontemps, *Black Thunder*
1937 Death of Bessie Smith 'Empress of the Blues'		**1937** Zora Neale Thurston, *Their Eyes were Watching God*
1939-45 Second World War		
	1940s Only black pupil at Lorain High School	**1940** Richard Wright, *Native Son*
		1941 *Twelve Million Black Voices*
1945 Birth of Jimi Hendrix		**1945** Richard Wright, *Black Boy*
	1949 Studied Classics and English at Howard University	**1949** Langston Hughes, *One-Way Ticket*
1950s McCarthy condemns Robeson as 'Communist'		
		1953 Richard Wright, *The Outsider*; James Baldwin, *Go Tell it on the Mountain*
1954 Supreme Court outlaws segregation in USA		
	1955 Masters degree in English from Cornell University; marries Harold Morrison, architect	**1955** James Baldwin, *Notes of a Native Son*
1957 Federal troops enforce integration, Arkansas		
		1960 Death of Richard Wright
1962 James Meredith, first black student at University of Mississippi; riots		

Events	Author's life	Literary world
1963 Martin Luther King's speech; 'I have a dream...'		**1963** James Baldwin, *The Fire Next Time*
1964 Civil Rights Act; assassination of President Kennedy; Nelson Mandela sentenced to life imprisonment	**1964** By now has two sons; marriage ends; becomes Senior Editor Random House publishers, New York; during this period publishes *The Black Book*	
1965 Voting Right Act; Malcolm X shot; race riots; 25,000 in Alabama civil rights march		
1966 Balck American soul music reaches cultural peak: Sam Cooke, Otis Redding, Aretha Franklin		
1968 Assassination of Martin Luther King		
1970 Death of Louis 'Satchmo' Armstrong	**1970** *The Bluest Eye*	**1970** Maya Angelou, *I Know Why the Caged Bird Sings*
	1970s (early) Reviews for *New York Times*	
	1974 *Sula;* teaches African English Literature at SUNY/Purchase, Yale University	
	1977 *Song of Solomon*	
1980 c. 26 million blacks, USA		
	1981 *Tar Baby*	
	1987 *Beloved*	**1987** Death of James Baldwin
	1988 Pulitzer Prize	
1990 Apartheid ban lifted; Mandela set free		
	1992 *Playing in the Dark* (criticism); *Jazz*	**1992** Darryl Pinckney, *High Cotton*
	1993 Nobel Prize for Literature	
	1998 *Paradise;* currently R.F. Gohoen Professor, Council of Humanities, Princeton University	

alliteration a sequence of repeated consonantal sounds in a stretch of language. The matching consonants are usually at the beginning of words or stressed syllables

allusion passing references. Morrison, through her many allusions to the pain of losing contact with one's children, strengthens an aspect of the destructive power of slavery

analogy a literary parallel. An analogy is a word, thing, idea or story which can help to explain whatever it is similar to: for example, schoolteacher's choice of analogies to explain Sethe's behaviour involve comparing her to a dog or horse (p. 149)

assonance the correspondence or near correspondence in two words of the stressed vowel, and sometimes those which follow, but, unlike rhyme, not of the consonants. It is the vowel equivalent of alliteration

associative the sometimes arbitrary relationship between ideas in the mind, used by psychoanalysts to explore the subconscious. Stream of consciousness narratives are associative in both form and narrative structure

asyntactic language that is lacking full grammatical arrangement

cathartic the 'purging' effect of tragic drama on the audience (a term devised by Aristotle)

canon, canonicity the Canon has come to mean the collected 'great works' of literature. Morrison, by virtue of her race and sex, would not in theory qualify for a place in this collection and the content and form of her works threaten many of its established values

oontoxtuali008 to put in context

dénouement the final unfolding of a plot

dialogic texts which allow the expression of a variety of points of view, in the manner of dialogue in drama, leaving the reader with open questions

eponymous the character of a book whose name is used as its title

interior monologue an attempt to convey in words the process of consciousness or thought

intertextual a term invented by the French critic Julia Kristeva to refer to the many and various kinds of relationship that exist between texts. Intertextual readings of

Beloved have included examining it in terms of the Gothic and comparing it to nineteenth-century white American texts such as *The Scarlet Letter* (1850) and *The Adventures of Huckleberry Finn* (1885)

irony saying one thing but conveying another meaning

juxtaposition placing side by side

lexical relating to items of vocabulary in a language

linear narrative narrative recounted chronologically

metaphor the description of one thing as another thing

multi-accentuality the capacity of words to have different meanings according to the contexts in which they are used. Words, far from having a fixed signification, may be the focus of conflict, for example, the implications of the word 'nurse' as used by Sethe

onomatopaeia words that sound like the noise they describe

paradox an apparently self-contradictory statement, or one that seems in conflict with all logic and opinion; yet lying behind the superficial absurdity is a meaning or truth

paratactic the placing of clauses, sentences or propositions side by side without connecting words

polyphonic (music) where two or more strands (instruments or voices) sound simultaneously. Different points of view allowed to co-exist rather than being organised to support a single authorial position

polysemous the capacity of words to have several separable meanings

protagonist the leading character in the novel

signifier according to Saussure words are considered as signs made up of two elements, the '**signifier**' (the noises, or marks on the paper, which constitute the sign) and the '**signified**' (the meaning to which the sign refers)

stream of consciousness an attempt to convey all the contents of a character's mind – memory, sense perceptions, feelings, intuitions, thoughts – in relation to the stream of experience as it passes by, often at random

symbol mark, token, sign

synecdoche a figure of speech in which a part is used to describe the whole of something or vice versa. In *Beloved*, 'mossy teeth' comes to stand for schoolteacher's nephews and also for white oppressors in general

synonym a word with a meaning identical to another word

tokenism the impropriety of drawing too many assumptions about African-American literature in its entirety after reading one text

zeugma words or phrases with different meanings are linked with comic effect by being made syntactically dependent on the same word, often a verb

AUTHOR OF THIS NOTE

Laura Gray is the author of the York Note on *Roll of Thunder, Hear My Cry* by Mildred D. Taylor. She was born in Scotland and studied English at Somerville College, Oxford. She is currently working in Italy.

NOTES

NOTES

NOTES

NOTES

NOTES

NOTES

NOTES

York Notes Advanced (£3.99 each)

Margaret Atwood
The Handmaid's Tale

Jane Austen
Mansfield Park

Jane Austen
Persuasion

Jane Austen
Pride and Prejudice

Alan Bennett
Talking Heads

William Blake
Songs of Innocence and of Experience

Charlotte Brontë
Jane Eyre

Emily Brontë
Wuthering Heights

Geoffrey Chaucer
The Franklin's Tale

Geoffrey Chaucer
General Prologue to the Canterbury Tales

Geoffrey Chaucer
The Wife of Bath's Prologue and Tale

Joseph Conrad
Heart of Darkness

Charles Dickens
Great Expectations

John Donne
Selected Poems

George Eliot
The Mill on the Floss

F. Scott Fitzgerald
The Great Gatsby

E.M. Forster
A Passage to India

Brian Friel
Translations

Thomas Hardy
The Mayor of Casterbridge

Thomas Hardy
Tess of the d'Urbervilles

Seamus Heaney
Selected Poems from Opened Ground

Nathaniel Hawthorne
The Scarlet Letter

James Joyce
Dubliners

John Keats
Selected Poems

Christopher Marlowe
Doctor Faustus

Arthur Miller
Death of a Salesman

Toni Morrison
Beloved

William Shakespeare
Antony and Cleopatra

William Shakespeare
As You Like It

William Shakespeare
Hamlet

William Shakespeare
King Lear

William Shakespeare
Measure for Measure

William Shakespeare
The Merchant of Venice

William Shakespeare
Much Ado About Nothing

William Shakespeare
Othello

William Shakespeare
Romeo and Juliet

William Shakespeare
The Tempest

William Shakespeare
The Winter's Tale

Mary Shelley
Frankenstein

Alice Walker
The Color Purple

Oscar Wilde
The Importance of Being Earnest

Tennessee Williams
A Streetcar Named Desire

John Webster
The Duchess of Malfi

W.B. Yeats
Selected Poems

GCSE and equivalent levels (£3.50 each)

Maya Angelou
I Know Why the Caged Bird Sings

Jane Austen
Pride and Prejudice

Alan Ayckbourn
Absent Friends

Elizabeth Barrett Browning
Selected Poems

Robert Bolt
A Man for All Seasons

Harold Brighouse
Hobson's Choice

Charlotte Brontë
Jane Eyre

Emily Brontë
Wuthering Heights

Shelagh Delaney
A Taste of Honey

Charles Dickens
David Copperfield

Charles Dickens
Great Expectations

Charles Dickens
Hard Times

Charles Dickens
Oliver Twist

Roddy Doyle
Paddy Clarke Ha Ha Ha

George Eliot
Silas Marner

George Eliot
The Mill on the Floss

William Golding
Lord of the Flies

Oliver Goldsmith
She Stoops To Conquer

Willis Hall
The Long and the Short and the Tall

Thomas Hardy
Far from the Madding Crowd

Thomas Hardy
The Mayor of Casterbridge

Thomas Hardy
Tess of the d'Urbervilles

Thomas Hardy
The Withered Arm and other Wessex Tales

L.P. Hartley
The Go-Between

Seamus Heaney
Selected Poems

Susan Hill
I'm the King of the Castle

Barry Hines
A Kestrel for a Knave

Louise Lawrence
Children of the Dust

Harper Lee
To Kill a Mockingbird

Laurie Lee
Cider with Rosie

Arthur Miller
The Crucible

Arthur Miller
A View from the Bridge

Robert O'Brien
Z for Zachariah

Frank O'Connor
My Oedipus Complex and other stories

George Orwell
Animal Farm

J.B. Priestley
An Inspector Calls

Willy Russell
Educating Rita

Willy Russell
Our Day Out

J.D. Salinger
The Catcher in the Rye

William Shakespeare
Henry IV Part 1

William Shakespeare
Henry V

William Shakespeare
Julius Caesar

William Shakespeare
Macbeth

William Shakespeare
The Merchant of Venice

William Shakespeare
A Midsummer Night's Dream

William Shakespeare
Much Ado About Nothing

William Shakespeare
Romeo and Juliet

William Shakespeare
The Tempest

William Shakespeare
Twelfth Night

George Bernard Shaw
Pygmalion

Mary Shelley
Frankenstein

R.C. Sherriff
Journey's End

Rukshana Smith
Salt on the snow

John Steinbeck
Of Mice and Men

Robert Louis Stevenson
Dr Jekyll and Mr Hyde

Jonathan Swift
Gulliver's Travels

Robert Swindells
Daz 4 Zoe

Mildred D. Taylor
Roll of Thunder, Hear My Cry

Mark Twain
Huckleberry Finn

James Watson
Talking in Whispers

William Wordsworth
Selected Poems

A Choice of Poets

Mystery Stories of the Nineteenth Century including The Signalman

Nineteenth Century Short Stories

Poetry of the First World War

Six Women Poets

Chinua Achebe
Things Fall Apart

Edward Albee
Who's Afraid of Virginia Woolf?

Margaret Atwood
Cat's Eye

Jane Austen
Emma

Jane Austen
Northanger Abbey

Jane Austen
Sense and Sensibility

Samuel Beckett
Waiting for Godot

Robert Browning
Selected Poems

Robert Burns
Selected Poems

Angela Carter
Nights at the Circus

Geoffrey Chaucer
The Merchant's Tale

Geoffrey Chaucer
The Miller's Tale

Geoffrey Chaucer
The Nun's Priest's Tale

Samuel Taylor Coleridge
Selected Poems

Daniel Defoe
Moll Flanders

Daniel Defoe
Robinson Crusoe

Charles Dickens
Bleak House

Charles Dickens
Hard Times

Emily Dickinson
Selected Poems

Carol Ann Duffy
Selected Poems

George Eliot
Middlemarch

T.S. Eliot
The Waste Land

T.S. Eliot
Selected Poems

Henry Fielding
Joseph Andrews

E.M. Forster
Howards End

John Fowles
The French Lieutenant's Woman

Robert Frost
Selected Poems

Elizabeth Gaskell
North and South

Stella Gibbons
Cold Comfort Farm

Graham Greene
Brighton Rock

Thomas Hardy
Jude the Obscure

Thomas Hardy
Selected Poems

Joseph Heller
Catch-22

Homer
The Iliad

Homer
The Odyssey

Gerard Manley Hopkins
Selected Poems

Aldous Huxley
Brave New World

Kazuo Ishiguro
The Remains of the Day

Ben Jonson
The Alchemist

Ben Jonson
Volpone

James Joyce
A Portrait of the Artist as a Young Man

Philip Larkin
Selected Poems

D.H. Lawrence
The Rainbow

D.H. Lawrence
Selected Stories

D.H. Lawrence
Sons and Lovers

D.H. Lawrence
Women in Love

John Milton
Paradise Lost Bks I & II

John Milton
Paradise Lost Bks IV & IX

Thomas More
Utopia

Sean O'Casey
Juno and the Paycock

George Orwell
Nineteen Eighty-four

John Osborne
Look Back in Anger

Wilfred Owen
Selected Poems

Sylvia Plath
Selected Poems

Alexander Pope
Rape of the Lock and other poems

Ruth Prawer Jhabvala
Heat and Dust

Jean Rhys
Wide Sargasso Sea

William Shakespeare
As You Like It

William Shakespeare
Coriolanus

William Shakespeare
Henry IV Pt 1

William Shakespeare
Henry V

William Shakespeare
Julius Caesar

William Shakespeare
Macbeth

William Shakespeare
Measure for Measure

William Shakespeare
A Midsummer Night's Dream

William Shakespeare
Richard II

William Shakespeare
Richard III

William Shakespeare
Sonnets

William Shakespeare
The Taming of the Shrew

FUTURE TITLES (continued)

William Shakespeare
Twelfth Night

William Shakespeare
The Winter's Tale

George Bernard Shaw
Arms and the Man

George Bernard Shaw
Saint Joan

Muriel Spark
The Prime of Miss Jean Brodie

John Steinbeck
The Grapes of Wrath

John Steinbeck
The Pearl

Tom Stoppard
Arcadia

Tom Stoppard
*Rosencrantz and Guildenstern
are Dead*

Jonathan Swift
*Gulliver's Travels and The
Modest Proposal*

Alfred, Lord Tennyson
Selected Poems

W.M. Thackeray
Vanity Fair

Virgil
The Aeneid

Edith Wharton
The Age of Innocence

Tennessee Williams
Cat on a Hot Tin Roof

Tennessee Williams
The Glass Menagerie

Virginia Woolf
Mrs Dalloway

Virginia Woolf
To the Lighthouse

William Wordsworth
Selected Poems

Metaphysical Poets